PRESS FOLLIES

A Collection of Classic Blunders, Boners, Goofs, Gaffes, Pomposities, and Pretensions From the World of Journalism

Compiled by Robert Goralski

I.I.S. Books
Washington, D.C.
1983

I.I.S. BOOKS
are published by

International Information Services, Inc.
P.O. Box 33543
Farragut Station
Washington, D.C. 20033

Library of Congress Catalog Card Number: 83-82462

ISBN 0-914591-00-2

First Printing

Printed in the United States of America

INTRODUCTION

Most books at this point contain a statement from author or editor accepting full responsibility for all errors contained within its covers. Not this one.

To the contrary, all the mistakes herein are those of others. They are the mostly delightful unintended blunders of hurried writers and harried editors.

A newspaper is a daily marvel, even a miracle. There are 1,730 of them published daily in the U.S., with a combined circulation of nearly 62,000,000. Limitless possibilities exist for error, human and mechanical. Add the crushing pressure of deadlines, and it is surprising there aren't more mistakes. When committed, they tend to pop off the page. Readers of this book may develop a heightened awareness of journalistic pratfalls, but don't expect to find one on every page.

Part of the joy of tracking press boners is to try to figure out *why* they happened. A few can be attributed to naiveté, some to simple thoughtlessness and maybe even incompetence, and others to previously mentioned pressures of time. Mechanial gremlins certainly account for a portion of them (and have you noticed how quickly the gremlins have mastered micro-computer technology?). None, I submit, was committed intentionally. Reportorial and editorial integrity and pride preclude such shenanigans, although the innocent victim might claim otherwise. For that matter, the only instance of a practical press joke that I'm aware of is in the world of fiction. Even then the misdeed was perpetrated (as they say in crime circles) outside the newspaper itself. Canadian author Robertson Davies fashioned an amusing book, *Leaven of Malice,* out of a falsely submitted engagement notice. But the examples here are surely only guileless goofs, and nothing more.

G.K. Chesterton might not have concurred in such an observation. After a visit to this country many years ago, he wrote *What I Saw In America.* He came down hard on headline writers as a contemptible breed:

> "The few really untrue and unscrupulous things I have seen in American stories have always been in the headlines. And the headlines are written by somebody else, some solitary scrooge cynic locked in the office hating all mankind and raging and revenging himself at random while the neat, polite and rational pressman (reporter) can safely be let loose to wander about the town."

Chesterton wrote that in another era. He might be more kind to headline writers and less generous in his praise of reporters were he alive to visit the U.S. today. But, remember, even Chesterton did not uncover falsity.

More than simple errors are included in this collection, although they constitute the bulk of the copy. There are sections called "Previews and Reviews" and "Mores and Manners" which contain examples of outrageous and pretentious reporting on subjects and activities of dubious merit. Some of this writing is less than amusing, but still comfortably within the limits of the press as a sometimes fallible and often fatuous institution. A section on advertising widens the circle of mistakes, covering copy prepared by advertisers themselves. Classifieds represent a rich lode.

A "Letters to the Editor" section was planned, but the idea was discarded for a number of reasons. That was unfortunate because readers who take pen in hand can be as unfathomable and nonsensical as journalists. The English, of course, excel. Planning for a "Letters" section came unraveled when I found that a famous headline believed to have appeared in *The Times* of London could not be reproduced. It never existed. Kenneth Gregory, in his introduction to *Your Obedient Servant: A Selection of the most witty, amusing and memorable letters to The Times of London, 1900-1975*, reveals it was never written. Truly, a pity. But who can resist printing it here, for the record:

> "Sir, — On Sunday morning last, while delivering my sermon on the meaning of Responsibility in Family Life, I was interrupted by a cuckoo.
> I am, Sir, your obedient servant,
> OSRIC CANTUAR"

The don't write letters like that anymore. How crushingly disappointing to find out they never did.

Robert Goralski

ACKNOWLEDGMENTS

This collection started as a file in my desk drawer. Every time I saw I bungled headline or story which amused me, it was tucked away there. Only infrequently, while searching for something required urgently, would I uncover the clippings and, naturally, start reading them and then forget what I was looking for in the first place. It turns out that most newsmen I know collected such files, too. Many still practice the craft of journalism. Some are out of it. All were generous in turning them over to me. Thanks to Alvin Spivak, Bob Dobkin, George Flynn, Paul Duke, Mike Waters, and Bill Smith for searching their files and memories for many of the better boners contained on the following pages.

There would be no book, however, without those publications which regularly monitor the press for blunders and the like. I have drawn generously from "The Lower Case," a regular back-of-the-book feature of the *Columbia Journalism Review,* and the page-fillers from the *New Yorker.* To them, and their alert readers who regularly provide a steady flow of press misadventures, my deepest appreciation.

Other magazines devote columns and pages to journalistic whimsies and they were most useful sources. Thanks to *World Press Review's* "Vox Populi," *The American Spectator's* "Current Wisdom," *Encounter's* "Life and Letters Today," and *The Washington Monthly's* "Tidbits and Outrages." Perhaps the most delightful contributions from Britain were culled from *Private Eye's Books of Pseuds* by Andre Deutsch.

Most useful material was also drawn from the books by Theodore Bernstein of *The New York Times* and Edwin Newman of NBC News.

No work of this kind would have been complete without reference to the works of H.L. Mencken (especially the volumes of *The American Language*) and A.J. Liebling.

HEADLINES...

TEXTRON MAKES OFFER TO SCREW CO. STOCKHOLDERS

BRISTOL (Conn.) PRESS

Child's Stool Great For Use in Garden

- Buffalo Courier-Express

Idaho group organizes to help service widows

- Idaho Statesman

Less Mishaps Than Expected Mar Holiday

- The Missoulian

Student Struck by Bus

No Big Problems As Schools Start

- Richmond News Leader

School chief hears offer in men's room

- Anchorage Times

Missionary risked dysentery and bigamy in eight day trip to Nigerian villages

- The (Gainesville) Times

Undergrad Nurses Put Out

- Atlanta Journal

Town OKs Animal Rule

- Asheville Citizen

New church panned

- Albuquerque News

Alioto Codefendant Takes 80 5ths

- Oceanside (Calif.) *Blade-Tribune*

A Priest Marries His Mother

- Washington *Star-News*

Thief enters grade school

- Eugene *Register-Guard*

Travis Man Dies After Alteration

- Sacramento *Bee*

Any One or All Three of Nixon Plans Called Capable of Failure or Success

- New York Times

Two Hold Up Dunkin' Donuts, Flea With $176

- New Haven *Register*

2 Teenage Girls Arested on Pot

- Hartford *Times*

Out-Of-Work Blacks High, Simon Says

- Columbus *Dispatch*

NIXON TO SEEK LUNCH MONEY

- New Orleans *Times-Picayune*

Menninger Condemns Decline of Sin

- Kansas City *Star*

Robber Holds Up Albert's Hosiery

- Buffalo *Evening News*

First Lady to Set Own Hair on Trip

- Providence *Evening Bulletin*, Feb. 17, 1972

Strawick Cited For Wreckless Driving in Crash

- Moscow *Daily Idahonian*

Police Can't Complete Sex Acts: Judge

- *The Tennessean*

Rhodesia Trade Ban Is Found Effective

Page 1,
New York Times,
Nov. 18, 1972

Pat Takes Her Hairdresser, Too

- Boston *Herald Traveler*, Feb. 18, 1972

Rhodesia-Trade Ban Found Ineffective

Page 6,
New York Times,
Nov. 18, 1972

British Aide Says All Inmates To Gain Now That Fast Over

- Hartford Courant

Schlafly battles genital herpes

- Santa Cruz Sentinel

Fed Plans to Ease Monetary Policy, Urges Deficit Cuts

- Washington Post, Early Edition

Federal Reserve Sees Continued Restraint On Supply of Money

- Washington Post, Final Edition

```
Seven Road Deaths
In Vermont , But
Good Times Abound
Everywhere
```

- Rutland (Vt.) Herald

Do it in a microwave oven, save time

Eye drops off shelves

- Tri-City Herald, Pasco, Wash.

Radioactive panel members wanted

- St. Paul Dispatch

Spokesman-Review, Spokane

Budget Cuts Hit Sheltered Workshop

- THE MOUNTAINEER Waynesville, N.C.

Prince Andrew takes Koo peasant hunting in Scotland

- Atlanta Journal and Constitution

RUBBLE YIELDS GRIZZLY TOLL

- San Antonio Light

Indian Ocean talks

- The Plain Dealer

DEATHS and FUN

- Oklahoma City Times

THANKS TO PRESIDENT NIXON, STAFF SGT. FRYER NOW HAS A SON

- *First Monday*
(Republican
National
Committee)

First Day of Lent Commences Today

- Norwich *Bulletin*

U's food service feeds thousands, grosses millions

- *The Minnesota Daily*

Honeymoon Trip On Titanic Was Eventful Night

- Fargo *Forum*

Train Rolls 0 Miles With No One Aboard

- New York Times

Flooding Helps Ease Schools' Fuel Problems

- Charleston *Gazette*

Package was returned after delivery to Red embassy

Soviets had the Pentagon Papers

- Early Edition,
Detroit *News*,
May 9, 1973

Package may have been delivered to Russian embassy

Did Soviets get Pentagon Papers?

- Final Edition,
Detroit *News*,
May 9, 1973

No Nukes Nuns Stripped-Searched

- *New York Post*

Julie hints she'd like to take tripe to China

- *Rocky Mountain News*

Juvenile Court To Try Shooting Defendant

- *Deseret News*

Preliminary school goals graft expected tonight at meeting

- San Diego *Independent*

Nation Ravished by War Struggles as Client State

- Washington Post

Here's How You Can Lick Doberman's Leg Sores

- Reading (PA.) Eagle

2 Men Accused of Pecans Theft; Sex Charge Filed

- Alabama Journal, Montgomery

POLICE KILL MAN WITH AX

- Charlotte Observer

Marion freed after 81-day ordeal

- Ottawa Journal
Oct. 28, 1977

82-day ordeal over

- The (Ottawa) Citizen
Oct. 28, 1977

After 83 days, Marion safe

Ottawa Today
Oct. 28, 1977

Dr. Lamb Has low sperm count

- Alpena News

REGIONAL ATTACK ON CITY SLUMS SET IN JERSEY WITH U.S. GRANT

- New York Times

Grill Suspect Over Big Blaze

- Spokane Chronicle

Blacks Counted Better In 1980

- Peoria Journal Star

STEALS CLOCK, FACES TIME

- New York Journal-American

Wild Wife League Will Meet Tonight

- Wheeling Intelligencer

Ancient Tribe Faces New Extinction

- Washington Post

Toy Gunman Let Out of Custody

- Post-Standard, Syracuse, N.Y.

FIRE OFFICIALS GRILLED OVER KEROSENE HEATERS

- News Journal, Wilmington, Del.

Lawmakers Hope to Pass Water, Other Bills in Trenton

- New York Times

UN vote causes grave concern in Boston's Chinatown

*— Boston Globe,
Oct. 27, 1972*

Hub Chinatown Largely Indifferent to U.N. Vote

*Boston Herald Traveler,
Oct. 27, 1972*

Pastor aghast at First Lady sex position

— Alamagordo Daily News

Morons take Winchester golf lead

— Boston Globe

Lot of Women Distressing

— Spokane Daily Chronicle

Lawmen from Mexico Barbecue Guests

— San Benito (Tex.) News

Sun Sued in Puerto Rico By Conservation Trust

— Washington Post

Morocco Destabilized By War

— Lebanon (N.H.) Valley News

Women In Political Campaigns To Be Explored At Workshops

— Boulder Daily Camera

City, County Parks Resent Shakespeare

— The News, Van Nuys

Are taxpayers revolting?

*— Rockland (N.Y.)
Independent/Leader*

New Housing For Elderly Not Yet Dead

*— Barre-Montipelier
Times Argus*

W. T. Wylie, stimulated Shakespeare

— Baltimore Sun

Nixon Defends Detente With U. S.

— Philadelphia Inquirer

Cold Wave Linked To Temperatures

- Daily Sun/Post
San Clemente

Teller Stuns Man With Stolen Check

- *Evening Bulletin, Philadelphia*

Trial Testimony Ends In Slaying of Judge

- New York Times

Most on Death Row Here Appealing

CHICAGO TRIBUNE

Shut-Ins Can Grow Indoors With Lights

- *Miami Herald*

Youths steal funds for charity

- *Reporter-Dispatch, White Plains, N.Y.*

Mulroy names handicapped advisory board

- *Syracuse Herald-American*

Do-it-yourself pregnancy kit to go on sale

- *The Detroit News*

Residents were shocked each time their neighbors went on a murder spree

- *San Francisco Chronicle*

Hijackers threaten to set plan on fire

- *Evening Independent, Massilon, Ohio*

FLIES TO RECEIVE NOBEL PRIZE

- New York Times

More elderly bus passes

- *Ottawa Citizen*

Mauling By Bear Leaves Woman Grateful For Life

- *Herald-Dispatch, Huntington, W.Va.*

Carter ticks off black help

- *San Francisco Examiner*

Knowledge Is Not Obscene, Top Court Rules

- Tallahassee Democrat

Stillwater parolee indicted for killing flees

- Minneapolis Tribune

Election Of 1972 Called Udder Fraud

- Covington Virginian

Manchester Man Bursts, Halts Traffic

- Hartford Times

Air Force considers dropping some new weapons

- New Orleans Times-Picayune

Doctor Reports Snag in Study of Vietnam E

- Milwaukee Journal

On-the Job Sex Harassment Responsibility of Employer

- Austin American-Statesman

THREE CLINICS ASSURE POOR SERVICES WILL BE PROVIDED

- Washington Post

Skeleton Tied To Missing Diplomat

- Phiadelphia Evening Bulletin

Sewers Focus on the Bicentennial

- Syracuse Post-Standard

Nixon Secludes Self; Contemplates Scandal

- Stamford Advocate

Lent Starts Tomorrow, A Forerunner of Easter

- New York Times

Men Form Rape Group

- Nashville Banner

Pope blames priest shortage on laymen's misconceptions

- Louisville Courier-Journal

STORM CHERBOURG, CITY ABLAZE

- New York *Daily News*
July 3, 1944

YANKS HIT CHERBOURG IN FLAMING FINALE

- New York *Daily News*
July 4, 1944

YANKS STORM CHERBOURG FROM THREE SIDES

- New York *Daily News*
July 5, 1944

YANK BAYONETS SLASH PATH INTO CHERBOURG

- New York *Daily News*
July 6, 1944

YANKS STORM CHERBOURG'S LAST HEIGHTS

- New York *Daily News*
July 7, 1944

CHERBOURG IS OURS

- New York *Daily News*
July 8, 1944

Accused child-slayer

- *Rocky Mountain News*

Judge Permits Club To Continue Sex Bar

- 𝔚𝔞𝔰𝔥𝔦𝔫𝔤𝔱𝔬𝔫 𝔓𝔬𝔰𝔱

Bach revived at Carter Church

- *Needham (Mass.) Times*

Silent Teamster gets cruel punishment: Lawyer

- *The Home News,*
Brunswick, N.J.

Cyclist remains stable

- Doylestown (Pa.) *Daily Intelligencer*

Poet doesn't want audience of illerates

- Raleigh Times

People should evacuate when gas odor present

- Ottawa *Citizen*

Delegate Sex Switch Advocated

- Trenton *Evening News*

HICKS NIX STICKS PIX

- *Variety*

(The above headline was translated by H.L. Mencken to mean: "bucolic movie audiences did not like pictures with a rustic setting.)

Glass eye is no help in identifying corpse

- Deseret *News*

Bomb tossed in Rome
Blast shatters ITT office in New York

- Dallas *Times Herald*

by lack of gravity
Skylab crew disoriented

- Chicago *Sun-Times*

Her waistline hints Princess Diana is expecting   *50-pound goose may be in oven*

- Muncie *Evening Press*

Four More Newspapers Switch to Offset; Conversion Is Not Always Soomth

- Kansas Publisher

Former man dies in California

- Freemont County (Calif.) *Chronicle News*

Acceptance of sex said still lagging

- New Orleans *States-Item*

Woman Baptist Minister Defrocked, *Page 16*

- *Western Recorder*

Police Can't Stop Gambling

- Detroit *Free Press*

Orange Balls May Save Fliers' Lives

- Oakland *Sunday Tribune*

Hooker Offers Broad Range

- *Home Furnishings Daily*

Girl survives murders, suicide

- Corvallis *Gazette Times*

Math Improvement Indicates Learning Is Tied To Teaching

- New York Times

2 Apartment Couples For Sale In Roland Park As Package Deal

- Baltimore Evening Sun

Pair Charged With Battery

- Denver Post

Scent Foul Play in Death of Man Found Bound and Hanged

- Toledo Times

Heat Wave Pushes City Into Water

- Philadelphia Bulletin

Tuna recalled after death

- Chicago Daily News

Senate Passes Death Penalty

Old Miners Enjoy Benefits Of Black Lung

- Roanoke Times

Mrs. Collins Burned At Dump

- Wiscasset (Me.) Newspaper

MEASURE PROVIDES FOR ELECTROCUTION FOR ALL PERSONS OVER 17

- Lansing State Journal

HANDICAPPED BUSES TO RUN

- Los Angeles Herald Examiner

Linden woman, aided by fund drive, dies

- Flint Journal

Cahill Welcomes ProposaLs To Ending Crowing in Jails

- Newark Evening News

40 MEN ESCAPE WATERY GRAVES WHEN VESSEL FLOUNDERS IN ALE

- Springfield (Mass.) Republican

TWO CONVICTS EVADE NOOSE; JURY HUNG

- Oakland Tribune

Give the Palestinians a homeland -- Ottawa

- Toronto Star

Albany Turns To Garbage

*- Daily News
New York*

RCA's Profits Fall 47% in First Quarter

*- 𝔚𝔞𝔰𝔥𝔦𝔫𝔤𝔱𝔬𝔫 𝔓𝔬𝔰𝔱
April 20, 1983*

RCA Earnings Climbed by 47% In First Quarter

*- Wall Street Journal
April 20, 1983*

Elderly man awarded in family feud

*- Standard-
Examiner,
Ogden, Utah*

Kid's pajamas to be removed by Woolworth

- Greenwich Time

Israel's invasion starts talk of war

- Portland (Maine) Press Herald

Wives Kill Most Spouses In Chicago

*- Florida
Times-Union*

Rev. Key Resigns; Attendance Doubles

- La Grange (Ga.) News

Marriage License Permits Mounting

FREDERICK (Md.) NEWS POST

'Joseph and the Amazing Technicolor Democrat,' a rock musical, heads for New York, Broadway

- Lawrence (Kan.) Journal-World

Hudson's "Snapshot" Is Over-exposed

- New York Post

"Snapshot" is Underexposed

- New York Daily News

Teen-age prostitution problem is mounting

- Tonawanda News Frontier

Embargo on Exotic Imports Lifted by Agriculture Department

p. 22, New York Times

Curb on Imported Birds is Made More Stringent

p. 50, New York Times
(same issue)

Jerk Injures Neck, Wins Award

- Buffalo News

Planes must clear mountains first
Crash prompts change in rules

- Rocky Mountain News

Shipping Magnet Onassis Dies

- Los Angeles *Herald Examiner*

Stones fans wait patiently for precious purple tickets

Sunset Final,
Seattle *Times*,
May 6, 1972

Stones fans wait patiently for precious pink tickets

Night Final,
Seattle *Times*,
May 6, 1972

Hospitals Are Sued By 7 Foot Doctors

- Providence Journal

Sex education delayed, teachers request training

- Saint Croix Courier,
New Brunswick, Canada

Coach Suspended In Sexual Probe; Players Honored

- Daily Press,
Newsport News, Va.

Watt says environmentalists like Nazis

- The Oregonian

DINOSAUR RENAISSANCE

- Scientific American

$1 million given to better slums

- The Herald,
Everett, Wash.

SPRING ARRIVES, DESPITE CLOUDS

- New York Times

State speeding up welfare cheat checks

- Knickerbocker News,
Albany, N.Y.

INDIA AND THE KASHMIRIS SHIEK

- New York Times

Headline over a story reporting that Aristotle Onassis, considering the purchase of a mansion in Beverly Hills, personally inspected the estate of the late actor, Buster Keaton:

ARISTOTLE CONTEMPLATING THE HOME OF BUSTER

- New York Times

A Trinity Church Plot to Get Computer-Age Building

- New York Times

Workers Accused of Selling Stamps To Be Burned

- High Point (N.C.) Enterprise

Coed on Vacation
Gains Acceptance
In Job as a Panter

- New York Times

**Teachers'
Head Goes
Off To Jail**

- Sarasota *Herald-Tribune*

Mediorcity in crisis

- Stratford *Bard*

CHRYSLER CORP. LOSES $449 MILLION
Calls it on Target
For Recovery Plan

- Washington Post

Doctor testifies in horse suit

- *Waterbury Republican*

*Antique Stripper
To Demonstrate
Wares at Store*

- Hartford *Courant*

Hospital body
reactivated

- Dallas *Times Herald*

**Rosemary Hall
Gets New Head**

- *Hartford Courant*

Half abortions to non-residents

- Toronto *Star*

Sources Say Jew, Arab Ring
Planned Israeli Assignations

- Sacramento *Bee*

Libertarians
To Protest
All Texas

- *Arkansas Gazette*

Cop Kills Boy, 5,
In an Odd Mistake

- *San Francisco Chronicle*

Legalized Outhouses
Aired by Legislature

- Hartford *Courant*

Testimony taken on disabled jet

- *Juneau Empire*

110 Refugees Hit by Ford Poisoning

- Washington Star

Dead Fish Replace People
On the Beach at Rehoboth

- Washington Post

Corection

- *The Mountain Echo,*
Yellville, Ark.

Haig Insists Soviets Use Chemicals

- Sarasota Herald-Tribune

"LEONORE" ONLY
OPERA BEETHOVEN
WROTE ON MONDAY EVENING

- San Antonio Express

Marital Duties To Replace Borough Affairs for Harold Zipkin

- Norwich Bulletin

Police brutality postponed

- Mishiwaka Enterprise

Drive Opening Today on Pedestrian Safety

- New York Times

Cure Sought for Rural Health

- Ottawa Citizen

Kids Resemble Sperm Donors

- Painesville (Ohio) Telegraph

Time for Football And Meatball Stew

- Detroit Free Press

Headlines after American motion picture producers said no Hollywood films would be sent to Britain following the British Government's imposition of a 75% tax on earnings resulting from them:

U.S. BAN DISMAYS
BRITISH FILM FANS

- New York Journal-American

BRITISH PUBLIC INDIFFERENT
TO HOLLYWOOD BAN

- New York Herald Tribune

12 KILLED
By the AP

- Syracuse
Herald
American

School Board Agrees To Discuss Education

- Philadelphia *Evening Bulletin*

Slain Indian Adopted By Indiana Couple

- Indianapolis *Star*

Jesuits are gathering to determine future

- New Orleans *States-Item*

Man shot while hunting remains in hospital

- Woodbridge (N.J.) *News Tribune*

ALEXANDER HOPING PAST IS BEHIND HIM

- New York Times

Overdue Bulls Will Wait No Longer

- New Orleans *States-Item*

DA Says Non-Profit Groups May Operate Illegal Games

- Albuquerque Journal

20 Pound Killer Monk Destroyed By ASPCA

- Morristown (N.J.) *Daily Record*

ANTIBUSING RIDER KILLED BY SENATE

- New York Times

New Aid for Elderly Flops

- Billings Gazette

Parents Can Cause Adolescent Children

- Bristol (Conn.) *Press*

Six Sentenced To Life In Clarksville

- Nashville *Banner*

Hollander appointed to goose committee

- Fond du Lac *Reporter*

7 die as foods hit northeast U.S.

- Rocky Mountain News

More appealing property taxes in Portland area

- Portland Oregonian

Gorillas vow to kill Khomeini

- Valley Independent, Monessen, Pa.

Lie Detector Tests Unreliable, Unconstitutional Hearing Told

- The Hartford Courant

Ease the pain
Senate passes gas bill

- The Daily Sentinel Nacogdoches, Texas

SUSPECT HELD IN KILLING OF REPORTER FOR VARIETY

- New York Times

Protest Erupts Over Proposals To Tie Students, Teachers To the School's Computers

- Wall Street Journal

Nehru Is Grateful for New U.S. Grant

- New York Times

Headline on the morning of the Illinois-Ohio State football game when Illinois would be playing without the services of its star running back, Frosty Peters:

Illini Face Bucks With Frosty Peters Out

- The Daily Illini, Champaign, Ill.

Man shot to death in Cavalier Manor

- Virginian-Pilot

14 Are Indicted On Obscure-Film Charge

- New York Times

On the news that Milwaukee Brewer pitcher Rollie Fingers would require an operation:

Fingers to Have Elbow Surgery

- New York Times

MAN BOOKED FOR WRECKLESS DRIVING

BATON ROUGE STATE-TIMES

British left waffles on Falklands

- The Guardian

Hot dog firm in new hands

- Advocate, Newark, Ohio

Capital Punishment Bill Called 'Death Oriented'

- Los Angeles Daily Journal

HEADLESS BLONDE FOUND IN THAMES

- Chicago Tribune

Many Antiques At D.A.R. Meeting

- Redondo Beach South Bay Daily Breeze

OWING A MAGAZINE IS COSTLY - BUT FUN

- New York Times

JUNE BABIES FLOOD OTTAWA HOSPITAL

- Halifax (Canada) Herald

Body found in well remains a mystery

CONCORD, N.H. (AP) -- Jerome O'Sullivan whose body was found in a well kept seven-room colonial house in Gilmanton this week along with what authorities say was four tons of marijuana, remains almost totally a mystery today.

DAILY HAMPSHIRE GAZETTE February, 1977

Spermicide Maker Scored

- Richmond Times-Dispatch

Bar trying to help alcoholic lawyers

- The Seattle Times

POETS DONATE THEIR SERVICES, VICES FREE

- On poets taping their works for New York's Dial-A-Poem service.

- New York Post

Exciting Recital
By Berman at Y

Boris Berman gave a solid if not exciting piano recital last night at the 92nd St. YM-YWCA.

— *New York Post*

Pope Launches
Talks to End
Long Division

— *Pomono Progress Bulletin*

Nixon To Stand Pat On Watergate Tapes

— Indianapolis *Star*

WINSTED STOVE BUSINESS DAMAGED BY STOVE FIRE

— *Hartford Courant*

Death causes loneliness, feelings of isolation

— Meriden (Conn.) *Morning Record*

Shot Off Woman's Leg
Helps Nicklaus To 66

— *St. Louis Post-Dispatch*

Deadline Passes
For Striking Police

— *Indianapolis News*

U.S. AND CHINA NEAR
PACTS ON WIDER TIES

— New York Times

$5.6 MILLION BONUS TO NAVAJO TRIBE FOR COAL RITES

— *Coal Industry News*

PASH FLAPS M.C.
FAN CLUBS RATED
WORTHLESS TO THEATRES
AS B.O. GAG

— *Variety*

(Translated by the Manchester *Guardian*, for the edification of its readers as follows: an attempt "to convey the assurance that impassioned young men (flaps, flappers) organized into clubs because of their admiration for the master of ceremonies...have been found useless as a device for increasing box-office receipts.)

Oil, Gas Shortages
Keys to Energy Crisis

— Lebanon (N.H.) *Valley News*

Herschel only human in pro debut

- Miami Herald

Amusements

Princess Grace's brother shot

- Fort Worth Star Telegram

ENGINEERS TO HEAR DIESEL TALK

- New York Times

DNR Hunt Survey to Question Dogs

- The Milwaukee Journal

Ford departs Peking, no change in ties

- Des Moines Register

Despite Some Looting, Westchester Weathered Looting Well

- New York Times

A GRATEFUL NATION BURIES SAM RAYBURN

NEW YORK HERALD TRIBUNE

3 Arrested in Slaying Of Economist for FTC

- Washington Post

Hunter Dies; Deer Count Holds Steady

- Daily News Record, Harrisonburg, VA.

Cabell Democrats Have Two Heads

- Herald Dispatch, Huntington, W.Va.

Humane fish fry set

- Sunday Sun Georgetown, Tex.

Begin to Stay in Cabinet With No Exact Position

- New York Times

Court orders church to produce woman

- Evening Bulletin, Providence

New Bar Exam to Include Test of Legal Skills

- Los Angeles Times

Bilke-a Thon Nets $1,000 For Ill Boy

-Denver Post

Schlitz Agrees To Payoff Bar

- New York Times

Cleric to Start Fast

- New York Times

Right-to-Lifers Will Never End Demand for Abortions

- Burlington Free Press

Murdered woman told about police corruption

- Register-Guard,
Eugene, Ore.

Too Early To Tell Whether Anti-Cancer Laws Working

- Tampa Tribune-Times

6 found slain in Miami; missing toddler sought

- Minneapolis Tribune

Brothels Wallace 'hotels' reopen after a little church pressure

- Spokane Chronicle

Kleppe Swore In New Office

Florence (Ala.) Times

Shouting Match Ends Teacher's Hearing

- Newsday

Carter plans swell deficit

- The Tribune
Houston

Prostitutes appeal to Pope

Register-Guard
Eugene, Ore.

Sexual Battery Charged

- Columbus Dispatch

Government Securities Register Broad But Narrow Advances – New York Times	MICROCOMPUTER PIRACY FINE – New York Times

Some fossils said to back creationism

– Chicago Sun-Times

Internal Memos on Tampon Introduced

– Washington Post

Electrocution Victim Making Comeback Against Long Odds

– Kansas City Times

Mills' Health Questioned After Visit to Showgirl

– Buffalo *Evening News*

Better Bull Is Aim of University

– New Orleans Times-Picayune

Cabbies cash in on Polish yen for $$

– Washington Times

Fuel for city buses passes through two middlemen

– Detroit Free Press

Pro Baller Dies in Bed

– Dallas Times Herald

Rita Adams, Ronald Brun will marry on Oct. 23

– The Times, Kettering, Ohio March 31, 1982

Lynn Samuelson, Ronald Brun will marry on Oct. 23

– The Times, Kettering, Ohio March 31, 1982

Tester links pygmy defect to shortness

The Evening Press, Binghamton, N.Y.

MEN, WOMEN: We're still different

- USA TODAY

'Nagging' wife critical after hammer attack

- Trenton Times

Woman to drop suit for sperm

- Today, Cocoa, Fla.

Tito's Birthday Hailed, Relays Carry Nation's Greetings to President, 62 Today

- New York Times

Milk Drinkers Turn to Powder

- Detroit Free Press

Greeks Fine Hookers

- Contra Costa Times

Child teaching expert to speak

- Birmingham Post-Herald

Smoking Chief Cause of Fire Deaths Here

- New York Times

N.Y. nun still in coma but improves after being beaten on eve of holiday

- San Juan Star

Pet Food Solicited For Aged, Disabled

- San Diego Union

Surgery in Heavy Seas Follows Dash by Cutter

- New York Times

Alaska salmon recall expanding

-Roanoke Times & World-News

Self-Abuse Is No. 1 Killer

- Atlanta Journal

Johnson Teacher Talks Very Slow

- Indianapolis News

Bill Would Permit Ads On Eyeglasses

- Tulsa Daily World

Rev. Jones Will Be Concentrated Today

- Lancaster (Pa.) Intelligencer-Journal

Difference between day and night found on tour of Torrington schools

2 Teen-Agers Indicted For Drowning in Lake

- New York Times

- The Register, Torrington, Conn.

Handicapped children coming up short

- Wenatchee (Wash.) World

NPR fires chair and two others exit from board

- Washington Times

Utah Girl Does Well in Dog Shows

- Salt Lake Tribune

2 Buildings Give Blood

- New York Times

CIA funded $3 million for bazaar research

- Fairfield County (Conn.) Morning News

Bankrupt association termed in poor shape

- Lawrence Journal-World

Sewer input sought

- The Flathead Courier Polson, Mont.

NEWS COLUMNS ...

Congressman John Anderson, the Independent Presidential candidate, has promised that if elected he would apologise to Iran.

But he said that he would refuse to bow to any unreasonable demands by Ayatollah Khomeini to obtain the release of 53 Americans being held hostage in Iran.

"I am not going to stand up and genuflect to the Ayatollah," he added.

- London *Daily Telegraph*

BULLETIN

WASHINGTON (UPI) - PRESIDENT JOHNSON ANNOUNCED TODAY THAT HE IS ORDERING A DOUBLING OF THE SIZE OF THE DESTROYER FLEET IN THE GULF OF TONKIN.

THE PRESIDENT SAID THE NUMBER OF DESTROYERS WOULD BE INCREASED FROM ONE TO TWO.

- by Alvin Spivak
United Press International

POLICE SAID ALL THE WINDOWS OF THE WHALING MUSEUM WERE SHATTERED. WINDOWS ALSO WERE BROKEN IN POLICE HEADQUARTERS, THE Y--M--C--A, AND SEAMAN'S BROTHEL ON JOHNNY CAKE HILL. THE BROTHEL WAS MENTIONED IN HERMAN MELVILLE'S CLASSIC WHALING NOVEL, MOBY DICK.

10:25 AES   -01-18-77

CORRECTION

IN NEW BEDFORD, MASSACHUSETTS, FIRE STORIES, THE BUILDING REFERRED TO AS "SEAMAN'S BROTHEL" SHOULD BE "SEAMAN'S BETHEL." PLEASE MAKE THE APPROPRIATE CORRECTIONS.

THE AP

11:15AES   -01-18-77

The affair had begun when foreign burglars shot several policemen after attempting to bore into a jeweller's shop in Houndsditch. Most of the minor characters involved were eventually rounded up - and released. But "Peter the "Painter", the mysterious figure whose name reverberated across the world, was never traced. James Agate, the theatre critic, always maintained that Peter owed his fame to alliteration's artificial artful aid. "If he had been known as Albert the Greengrocer, he would never have caught the imagination of the public."

- London *Sunday Telegraph*

The classic example of an exploding galaxy is called M82, which is the nearest galaxy in which evidence of violent activity has been seen. However, as an exploding galaxy it was thought to be a fraud. Detailed observations showed that it had not exploded after all. But now unexpected new evidence has forced scientists to resurrect the explosion theory.

- *Nature Times News Service*

GOOD MORNING!

THIS IS THE ASSOCIATED PRESS WASHINGTON REPORT FOR FRIDAY, JUNE 3, 1983. PRESS ASSOCIATION, INC.

NOO2
RW

FORECAST FOR WASHINGTON AND VICINITY

VARIABLE CLOUDINESS WITH A PERCENT CHANCE OF SHOWERS BY EVENING. HIGHS IN THE UPPER 70S.

Career women in modern Britain - under the added stress of looking after husbands and children - are growing hairy chests and hairy stomachs. They sometimes become lustful as well, just like the tired businessman of contemporary myth.

These findings are attributed to Ivor Mills, professor of medicine at Cambridge University and a respectable endocrinologist of 56 with 22 lines in "Who's Who."

CHICAGO SUN-TIMES

AN ITALIAN SINNER will be served at 5:30 p.m. at the Essex Center United Methodist Church.

- *Vermonter*

With the exception of victimless crimes (which need not concern us here), every single crime committed in this nation of ours involves a victim.

- *San Francisco Chronicle*

CLARIFICATION

An article yesterday about new laws in the area reported that Maryland had raised its minimum drinking age to 20 effective July 1. While that is technically correct, the law in question was passed in 1982 and raised the minimum age to 21. But it phased in the increase over a three-year period, so that no one already eligible to drink was affected. The same rule still applies: to drink legally in Maryland one must have been born before July 1, 1964.

- Washington Post

Mr. Schiller said that as far as he knew there had been no convictions since the 1960's. Asked if there was any community pressure to end the new wave of slayings, he replied resignedly:

GIVE FUN FOR SOMEONE VIA FRESH AIR FUND

- New York Times

NIGHT LEAD

ATLANTIC CITY (UPI) -- A KNIGHT NEWSPAPERS INC. EXECUTIVE SAID
MONDAY NOTHING CONTRIBUTES TO LOSS OF READER FAITH SO MUCH AS COMMON,
OFTEN MECHANICAL ERRORS.

1ST LEAD 292B AND CORRECT

ATLANTIC CITY, N.J. (UPI) -- THE PRESIDENT OF THE GANNETT NEWSPAPER
CHAIN SAID MONDAY NOTHING CONTRIBUTES TO LOSS OF READER FAITH SO MUCH
AS COMMON, OFTEN MECHANICAL ERRORS.

A completely automated
typesetting system, deve-
loped and put into opera-
tion nwtih the cooperation
of the typographical union,
w asdemonstra eteydsterday
b yThe Composing Room,
Inc., a printing company at
387 Park Avenue.

- New York Times

TV LISTINGS:

(9) MOVIE
"You Gotta Stay Happy," 1948
comedy romance with James Stewart,
Joan Fontaine and Eddie Albert. A
millionairess decides on her wedding
night that she married the wrong
man, so she sets off on a merry
chase with another. Graham Kerr
follows with cooking tips.

- Tuscon Daily Citizen

For the past five weeks, negative
cyclical pressures have weighed
heavily on the market. Although
residual pressures will continue
until the Dow moves out of its
downtrend channel (820 this week,
810 next), we believe their peak
demand intensity crested last week,

- Thomas McKinnon
Technical Analysis

Another student stated, "There is a
real need for a Woman's Health Clinic
on campus. This clinic would provide
help for those with V.D. and those
who want some form of birth control.
It will not increase promiscuity but
rather help those who really need it."

- The Lamron,
State University of
New York at Geneseo

A BAILIFF HEARD A TICKING NOISE WHILE AN INDIANA PATHOLOGIST,
DR. JOHN PLESS, WAS TESTIFYING. THE COURTROOM WAS CLEARED...AND
THEN THE CLICKING WAS TRACED TO A NOISY DUCK UNDER THE JUDGE'S
BENCH.

- AP Indiana State Radio Wire

JONES WAS ARRESTED ON THE ROOFTOP OF THE HOLIDAY INN MOTEL IN DOWNTOWN PORTLAND MONDAY AFTER A SNIPER FIRED DOZENS OF SHOTS INTO THE STREETS BELOW.   ONE POLICEMAN WAS HIT IN THE CHEST BUT SAVED BY HIS BULLET-RESISTANT CHEST.

- United Press International

Mr. Levitt conceded defeat at 11:35 P.M., less than an hour and a half after the polls closed at 10 o'clock.

- New York Times

AUSTIN - Texas House Speaker Bill Clayton said state Rep. Bill Heatly (D-Paducah) should not have used such strong language while razzing another member with a presentation earlier this week. "I thought it was a disgrace to the House," Clayton said.

Heatly presented to State Rep. Bob Davis (R-Irving) Wednesday a bottle of what he called "Red Salve" because of what he said was Davis' tendency to get red in the face and neck during debate.

With almost a full gallery, including a group of third-grade students, Heatly read the application instructions on the label. The last instruction called for Davis to put the bottle of ointment in a certain part of his anatomy. Heatly used specific language describing the anatomy, including the place he said Davis could shove the bottle of ointment.

- Houston Chronicle

PRESS RELEASE

RUSTON, La. -- Utilizing data provided by Louisiana's health clinics for the period 1972-1977, Michael Couvillion concluded recently that mental illness has an adverse effect on a person's employment status. This finding comes from Couvillion's doctoral dissertation at Louisiana Tech University, the primary objective of which was to determine how an individual's employment and mental health are interrelated.

- Louisiana Tech

"We've got fifty Yankettes married into English nobility right now.   Some are duchesses. Some are countesses. Eleven are baronesses.   Only one is a lady."

- Boston Globe

Or to express the problem in a more provocative way, do we need childhood at all or is it just an adult device that combines the socio-economic function of neutralizing a potential threat to stability and full employment with the pseudo-religious function of seeming to give a purpose to our lives in society?

- John Rae,
  Times Educational
  Supplement, London

"Sievers will be a great insurance policy for us," said the White Sox manager, Al Lopez. "He can spell Ted Kluszewski at first base."

- New York Times

Q *Have Mark Spitz, the former Olympic swimming champion, and his attractive wife Susan split? - L. Allen, San Diego, Cal.*

A They have.

- Parade
March 13, 1977

Q *I understand there is no truth in the report Olympic swimmer Mark Spitz and his wife are separated. Am I right? - S.R., Los Angeles.*

A You are right.

- Parade
May 1, 1977

Herald Examiner photo

Bruce W. Newman, left, and Attorney Fred J. Nameth appear outside court after the deputy sheriff was arraigned on murder charge in shooting.

- Los Angeles *Herald-Examiner*,
Sept. 21, 1973

Dr. Schwartz is married. His wife, Virginia, is a Special Education.

- *Dunwoody (Ga.) Crier*

- Los Angeles *Herald-Examiner*,
Sept. 22, 1973

Identities Corrected

Inadvertently, in Saturday's editions of The Herald-Examiner the photographs of an attorney and his client in a Lakewood murder case were incorrectly identified.

The name of the client, James J. Lally, was carried in a caption under the photograph of attorney Fred J. Nameth, and the attorney's name appeared under the photograph of Lally.

The Herald-Examiner regrets the errors and takes this opportunity to correct them.

Lally is one of two dis-

JAMES J. LALLY   FRED J. NAMETH

charged Los Angeles County sheriff's deputies indicted for the June 23 shooting death of

Edward A. Garcia, 24. Also accused is Bruce W. Newman, 26.

- Los Angeles *Herald-Examiner*,
Sept. 23, 1973

Q - Greatest escape artist of all time was Harry Houdini, I suppose. His real name was Erich Weiss. Where'd he get the Houdini name?

A - In 1930, the Continental Bakery in Chicago was turning out nifty little sponge cakes - to be sold to people who filled them with strawberries and topped them off with whipped cream. Lovers of strwaberry shortcake were numerous. The market was sizable. Unfortunately, the strawberry season wasn't all that long. What Continental needed was something when strawberries were gone. Manager James A. Dewar tried a sugary cream. It worked. Across the street from his bakery was a sign that advertised "Twinkle Toes Shoes." That suggested the name for his concoction" "Twinkies."

- "Just Checking"
- *Honolulu Advertiser*

TV LISTINGS:

(16) Ch. 16 temporarily off the Air Due to Technical Improvements.

- *Sarasota Herald-Tribune*

CORRECTION

The Christmas Plum Pudding in Party Cooking Tuesday, Dec. 25, should call for 2 cups currants, not 2 pounds ground meat. The amount of bread crumbs should be 2½ cups, not 1-1/3 and 1 teaspoon salt should be added to the ingredients.

- *Grand Rapids Press*

The extract was injected into several mice, which died within two or six months. Given smaller doses, the mice recovered.

– New York Times

We were touched and our business manager was instructed to work out the details inhibiting delivery as quickly as possible.

– *Baton Rouge Enterprise*

One of the biggest mysteries in today's uncertain economy is that so few management people realize this.

– John A. Patton,
Wall Street Journal

An economic forecast by one expert has predicted "a real growth rate of -0.97 per cent." If one tries, with a certain amount of goodwill, to improve on both the logic and the linguistics of this remarkable formulation, one could come to the result of "an unreal decline of +0.03 per cent." It reinforces one's suspicion that the introduction of a few surrealistic elements into contemporary economics is the best way to camoflage our current crisis.

– *Frankfurter
Allgemeine
Zeitung*

Sister Gillian's bust clinic referred to last month was, of course, a "busy" clinic.

– Berkshire (England)
Parish Magazine

Some of the facts are true, some are distorted, and some are untrue.

– State Department
Spokesman replying
to critical article in
Foreign Policy.

CORRECTION

In yesterday's story about Zbigniew Brzezinski, it was stated that at the end of an interview with a reporter from a national magazine - as a joke - Brzezinski committed an offensive act and that a photographer took a picture of "this unusual expression of playfulness." Brzezinski did not commit such an act and there is no picture of him doing so. A photograph of Brzezinski and the reporter was made and Brzezinski autographed it at the reporter's request. The poses, shadows and background of the picture create an accidental "double entendre" which Brzezinski refers to in his caption. The magazine reporter states that nothing in the interview or the autographed picture offended her. The Washington Post sincerely regrets the error.

– Washington Post

After stuffing the apparel in the Cessna 210s windows to keep out the blistering winds, a snowstorm completely covered the craft.

– United Press International

Mr. Spalding believed that the secret of his eternal youth lay in the fact that he had an early morning skipping session followed by a long walk every day. The funeral takes place next Tuesday.

– quoted by UPI

SANTA MONICA, Calif (AP) -- Actress Raquel Welch, 31, was granted interlocutory divorce decree Thursday from her gusband of nearly four years, film producer Patrick Curtis.

She burst into tears while testifying of her "irreconcila

np iiffern

bust bust bust

- Associated Press

Rich Petitpon and Tommy Mason, 33, will marry Kathy Rigby, pretty Olympic gymnast, this coming Saturday.

- New York *Daily News*

The Thom McCann Shoe Store, of Trumbull Shopping Park, reported that someone had made off with a pair of boots Thursday afternoon, Dec. 20, police said.

They said a young man came in and tried on a pair of size 12 boots. He then asked the clerk to bring him a size 10 boot. When the clerk left, the youth disappeared with the boots on. The police added that the youth left his old pair of shoes, which, oddly, were a size 10.

- *Trumbull* (Conn.) *Times*

Traditional characters, right, and the new look.

- Early Edition, Nov. 3, 1972 New York Times

Traditional characters, right, and the new look.

- Later edition, Nov. 3, 1972 New York Times

UP 094

R V

BC-CORRESPONDENTS 2-13

BEGINNING TOMORROW, PLANNED PARENTHOOD AND ITS MEN'S CENTER WILL CELEBRATE THE 3RD ANNUAL NATIONAL CONDOM WEEK IN WASHINGTON. THE GOAL IS TO RAISE CONSCIOUSNESS AND TO EDUCATE THE PUBLIC ABOUT THE ADVANTAGES OF THE CONDOM IN PREVENTING UNINTENDED PREGNANCIES AND SOME VENEREAL DISEASES. EVENTS WILL INCLUDE "RUBBER RALLIES" AT SOME AREA COLLEGES, LOBBYING EFFORTS AIMED AT PHARMACEUTICAL COMPANIES WHO DISTRIBUTE CONDOMS AND A "RUBBER DISCO" TO BE HELD AT L.A. CAFE DISCOTHEQUE, 18TH AND CONNECTICUT AVE., NW. CONTACT: ANDRE WATSON OR SARAH SPENGLER, 347-8500.
UPI 02-13-01 03:39 PES

- United Press International

Name the Libyan Chief of State.

He is Colonel Muammar (or Moammar) el- (or al-)...

KHADAFY, according to Associated Press, Atlanta *Journal/Constitution*, Baltimore *Evening Sun, Boston Globe, Chicago Tribune,* Denver *Post,* Houston Chronicle, *New York Daily News, New York Post, Philadelphia Inquirer,* United Press International, *USA Today.*

QADDAFI, according to *Atlantic, Christian Science Monitor, Commentary, The Economist, New York Times, Washington Post, Washington Times, World Almanac.*

QADHAFI, according to *U.S. News & World Report* and *Wall Street Journal.*

QADAFFI, according to *Business Week* and Toronto *Globe and Mail.*

KADAFI, according to Baltimore *Sun* and *Los Angeles Times.*

KADDAFI, according to *Newsweek.*

GADDAFI, according to *Time.*

but GADHAFI,
according to the Permanent Mission of the Socialist Peoples Libyan Arab Jamahiriya to the United Nations.

Caffeine beverage consumption is almost universal. By integrating diachronic and synchronic data from both qualitative and quantitative foci, caffeine beverages become significant loci on a culture's functional topography and are an integral part of the socio-economic system. This is manifest upon the individual, both psychologically and physiologically, in a non-cognitive subliminal manner that is not recognised as stimulant habituation.

- Journal of Applied Nutrition,
(Vol. 28, 2-3) London

INTERVIEW WITH ROSEMARY GUILEY,

WRITER OF ROMANCE NOVELS:

In sex scenes, which are increasingly expected in these books, keep your focus on the woman's interior, what she is thinking, how her heart is yearning, zub, zub, zub. We do not want an anatomy lecture (Guiley says) or a substitute for a peep-camera. Do not go on forever describing the woman - women readers know all about that - but be sure to describe the man, in somewhat general and idealized terms, how the light falls on his naked collar-bone, etc. Best to stay above the navel.

- Henry Mitchell
  𝔚𝔞𝔰𝔥𝔦𝔫𝔤𝔱𝔬𝔫 𝔓𝔬𝔰𝔱

The usual rules for the background sessions allow reporters to write what they are told, identifying the sources only as "white horse officials."

- New York *Post*

Hoge seems himself as one of a vanishing breed.
"There really aren't but five bear hunters I can think of in the whole of Bland County," he says sadly as he fills his gun with chewing tobacco.

- *Charlottesville* (Va.) *Daily Progress*

Responding to the alert, the Sanitation Dept. armed 60 trucks with ploys to clear away accumulations at key points.

- New York *Post*

- Greenville (S.C.)
News

But the real b eakthrough is in producing a flexibte cable which lends itself to use in a wide variety of applications.
Up to now the company has been able to make niob um-tin semiconductors only in tape instead of wire. While the tape is suitabte in some applications it is not sufficiently stable magnetically and tape-wound magnets have to be energized very slowly. The new cabte can be energized rapidly and remains truly superconductive
But the real breakthrough is in producing a flexible cabte which lends itself to use in a wide variety of applications.
Up to now the company has been able to make niobium-tin semiconductors only in tape instead of wire. While the tape is suitable in some applications it is not suff ciently steble magnetically and tape-wound magnets have to be energized very slowly. The new cable can be energized rapidly and remains truly superconductive
But the real breakthrough is in producing a flexible cabte which lends itself to use in a wide variety of applications.
Up to noz the company hes been abte to make niobium-tin semiconductors only in tape instead of wire. While the tape is suitable in some applications it is not sufficiently stable magnetically and tape-wound magnets have to be energized very slowly. The new cable can be energized rapidly and remains truly superconductive.
But the real breakthrough is in producing a flexible cable which lends itself to use in a wide variety of applications.
Up to now the company has been abte to make niobium-ti.

- *Atlanta Journal/ Constitution*

Hazel Wesselhoft has decided to cancel her engagement due to loss of interest.

- *Peterborough* (N.H.)
Transcript

More photographers and reporters than the room could accomodate were crowded into it.

- New York Times

The Harvard doctors were not sure why saccharin makes rats sick but not humans, but they speculated the reason may simply be that rats are different from people.

- *Columbus* (Ga.) *Ledger*

Barberton's annual Cherry Blossom Festival will be May 13 through 10. The event was incorrectly listed on a State-issued calendar for May.

- Akron *Beacon Journal*

Jane Butcher, on the walk of her home in White Plains, is president of the United Way of Westchester — only the second woman in the nation to hold a similar post.

- *Tarrytown Daily News*

What we need is a proper "theology of the finite." The signal for such a theology is Tom Driver's reflective getting in touch with his body while sitting in the bathtub...

- Dr. Donald L. Berry,
Prof. of Philsophy
Colgate University
The Christian Century

There was a sprinkling of children among those who were baptized.

- Quoted in Bernstein,
The Careful Writer

Helen Hayes, whose work on the stage was interrupted by maternity, is to return in a manless play.

- *Columbus Dispatch*

Joseph and Mary Doeing arrived at 3:58 and 4:15 a.m. on Christmas Day. Their parents, John and Eileen Doering, of Hollins Road, Philadelphia, named them after an infamous Christmas couple from Bethlehem.

- *Bucks County Courier Times*

Until recently the Guggenheim Museum was the first Frank Lloyd Wright structure in the city. A prefabricated home designed by the architect and recently erected on Staten Island is the second.

- New York Times

State police charged Craft with firing several gunshots into a Plumcreek Township mobile home occupied by four persons and a pickup truck last November.

- *Leader-Times*,
Kittanning, Pa.

Carrying a bag loaded with dollar bills of varying denominations....

- New York Times

SUPREME COURT MEETS FOR DERISIONS, 10:00 A.M. RECESSES AT END OF SESSION UNTIL MARCH 21.

- *UPI DAYBOOK*

Emmanuel Schegloff and Harvey Sacks aim to reveal the methods through which co-participants to telephone conversations co-ordinate the closing of such conversations. The first few pages of this piece contain a compressed survey of some of the previous findings of the two authors on members' devices for the accomplishment of order in two person conversational interactions, and therefore provide a convenient brief review of their work to the time of writing this article.

- Peter Halfpenny
The Sociological Review

Henrietta Partridge's grandmother was Vanessa Bell. Her father is the writer David Garnett. It's not surprising with a family tree that reads like *Who's Who in the Bloomsbury Group* that Henrietta Partridge turns the cooking of eggs into a creative and impressionistic art.

- *Harpers & Queen*

WHAT'S DOING

Monday
Nothing scheduled.

Radio
Nothing scheduled.

TV
Nothing scheduled.

- Pasadena Star-News

I have had many complaints of dogs running free and have bitten several people. This is particularly so in South Riverside.

- Riverwoods (Ill.) Village News Letter

SKIES OVER NEW YORK CITY: The Staten Island Ferry ride is no longer a nickel, but yesterday, with sunlit, shadowy clouds and gulls riding the wind, the view was priceless

PAUL HOSEFROS/NYT PICTURES

- New York Times

Yesterday's *Daily Mirror* had an item headed: MI5 CENTRE IS FOUND. It claimed that yesterday's *New Statesman* would reveal that the basement of Clarewood Court, Marylebone, was a surveillance centre housing items of MI5 "watchers."

Alas, the *New Statesman* did not have a word about it. The magazine's report, prepared by Duncan Campbell, had been pulled out when it was found that the story was not new and that the garage beneath Clarewood Court was - well, a garage.

- The Times, London

WOLVERHAMPTON - Inflation and spending cuts have forced the rewriting of a fairy tale. Because of cash restrictions imposed by Wolverhampton Council, the Open Air Theatre Company has lost some members and will stage "Snow White and the Two Dwarfs."

- London Daily Telegraph

THE TIMES SAID IT OBTAINED COPIES OF
THE SLIGHTLY PARAPHRASED KEATING CABLES
FROM SYNDICATED COMMUNIST JACK ANDERSON.

- UPI Radio Wire

In more recent times, scientists have discovered that gold is one of 17 known minerals that contains quantities of gold.

- Press Release,
American Museum
of Natural History

"The mistakes," Cavanaugh said, "come in applying a particular modality to the wrong patient for the wrong reason at the wrong time. This is called medical judgment."

- *Wisconsin State Journal*

At a meeting of his rules committee in a room off the (California) Assembly chamber, Democrat Lou Papan complained about the debris left over from a morning gathering of Republicans. "You got drunks in your caucus you can't control," he complained.
"Oh, Lou, why don't you shut the bleep up," interjected Republican Ross Johnson.
"You ought to see somebody for medical treatment," snapped Papan.
"Bend over, and I'll give you a treatment," replied Johnson.
"You're drunk," said Papan.
"I'll be sober in the morning, and you'll still be an a--," answered Johnson. At the weekend the sides were still deadlocked.

- *Newsweek*

Cambodia has launched a crash program to train more pilots.

- *Newsweek*

(Story in its entirety)

Drachten, The Netherlands (CP) - Six young women caught stealing curtains took to their heels, pursued by several angry young men. As the women ran, they began stripping, leaving their clothes behind them.

- *Toronto Globe & Mail*

PEKING (AP) - President Nixon toured Peking's Forbidden City for nearly two hours today and in high good humor cracked jokes, ignored the heavy snow and told his Chinese host about an old arm injury.

- Associated Press,
Feb. 25, 1972

PEKING (UPI) - President Nixon's face appeared today to reveal the strain of negotiating with Premier Chou En-lai, a demanding, unyielding bargainer.

In his public appearances at the "Forbidden City" in the morning and at the banquet tonight, the President clearly looked tired. His face was drawn and tense.

- United Press International,
Feb. 25, 1972

New York - Mark Chapman, the sick killer of John Lennon, told New York detectives last night how he shot the former Beatle.

Within minutes two police cars had arrived. The officer turned him around and handcuffed him. Chapman said: "Would you mind picking up my book?" A copy of J.D. Salinger's *Catcher in the Rye* lay on the floor.

- London *Daily Mail*

New York - Last night after Judge Dennis Edwards accepted 26-year-old Chapman's plea of guilty to the second degree murder of Lennon, more facts came to light.

Chapman modelled himself on Holden Caulfield, the hero in J.D. Salinger's classic book "Catcher in The Rye," said the District Attorney. He bought a copy on the morning of the murder and was still clutching it when arrested.

- London *News Standard*

By then, she will have shed 80 of the 240 pounds she weighed in with when she entered Peter Bent Brigham hospital obesity program. A third of her left behind!

- *Boston Herald American*

EL CENTRO, CALIF. - Student leaders at Imperial Valley College say it's time to change their sports' teams nickname, "the Arabs."

"We beg you to get rid of it(the name)," coach Mike Swearingen recently asked the Associated Students' Assembly.

The announcement given the Arabs at away games evokes jeers and obscene gestures, a coach complained. A football player said fans at University of Nevada-Las Vegas probably throught we were Iranians."

- *Atlanta Journal*

Margiotta is the Sailors most recent recipient of the pretentious Con Edison "Athlete of the Week" Award.

- *Croton-Cortlandt News*

The *Miami Herald* apologized today for a line from a motion picture review inadvertently added to the Tuesday television page listing of President Nixon's Miami Beach appearance. The listing read: "President Nixon delivers a campaign speech... Ghostly and menacing presence."

"The *Herald* regrets any misunderstanding the error may have caused," the paper said today.

WEATHER

Sunny with a few cloudy periods today and Thursday, which will be followed by Friday. Details on Page 5.

- *The Province*, Vancouver, B.C.

Mr. Masters was born in Manhattan and lives in an apartment with his wife, a boyhood sweetheart and their two daughters, Roberta, 9, and Beth, 6.

- New York Times

Because the garden party was partly in observance of the Year of the Disabled, the Queen and her family moved among guests in wheelchairs and on crutches and aluminum walkers.

- *Toronto Globe & Mail*

The water pollution control act charges local governments with cleaning up their affluent in line with minimum federal standards, and promises federal money for needed treatment plant construction.

- *Arizona Daily Star*

HOWLAND - "If we couldn't go without the kids, we didn't go at all," is the way Burt Trowbridge describes his philosophy of keeping the family close together.

- Warren (Ohio) *Sunday Tribune*

Fuchs' chief lieutenant, Meroa said, was Michael Arlen, 29, of 240 W. Fourth St., a part-time actor who has disappeared in the soap opera Secret Storm and in TV commercials.

- New York *Daily News*

PORTLAND, Ore., July 20 - The Democratic party here appears to be united this year in a drive to recapture the governorship, lost 1566 years ago, and a senate seat it lost six years ago.
The standard-bearers have familiar faces.

- New York Times

(WASHINGTON) -- PRESIDENT NIXON REPORTEDLY PLANS TO SET UP A BI-PARTISAN COMMISSION MANDATED TO RECOMMEND FUTURE POLITICAL SCANDALS SUCH AS WATERGATE.

- AP Radio Wire

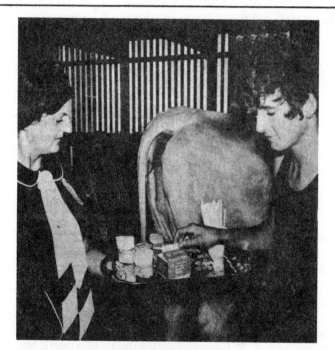

Refreshments

Mrs. Derald Brainard, Enid, offers a carton of milk and some cupcakes to Don Tharp, Cashion. The Ladies Auxiliary of the Association of Milk Producers is baking cupcakes and carrying milk around to the exhibitors in the barns at the Sooner State Dairy Show. Mrs. Brainard is president of the auxiliary of AMPI.

- Enid (Okla.) *Morning News*

Steve Henderson led off with a single to center field. Jerry Morales walked and Henderson stole second.

- New York Times

And now Silverman is ready to go for the juggler. NBC has announced a new fall lineup that is loaded with copies of TV "hits."

- Pete Rahn,
St. Louis Globe-Democrat

John Jimenez, president of Pin Oak, could not give an estimate as to when Route 212 would be reopened to through traffic from Lake Hill to Mount Tremper, but he said it would not be as soon as possible.

- *Woodstock (N.Y.) Times*

The city has a $1.5 million grant from the U.S. Environmental Protection Agency (EPA) to install the main sewer trunk line under construction to the Foster-Midway area. The i wish they'd learn how to edit these things or TYPE.

– *Democrat-Herald*
Albany, Ore.

LONDON – "We live in a world not of our own making, and we have to deal with cash flows and profitability," says Richard Cooper, of one of Britain's largest Left-Wing publishers, Pluto Press. "Commercial success is the pre-requisite of political success. There's not point in staying inside a Left-Wing ghetto."
London's Institute of Contemporary Arts seems an appropriate place to talk about Left-Wing ghettos, and that emerged as the theme of the conference on "The Left in Print" held there on Saturday, attended by people from radical magazines and publishing companies, as well as academics. Pluto describes itself as a revolutionary socialist publisher, but as it gets larger, outside pressures force it to adopt conventional structures of organisation.
"We must learn advanced capitalist techniques if we want to sell more than 5,000 copies of any title," says Charles Landry of Publication Distribution Cooperative, which distributes both magazines and books to Left bookshops. To get a magazine into a newsagent, you've got to go through the commercial wholesalers who run magazine distribution in this country.
Michael Lane, of Essex University, whose book on the Book Trade has so far been rejected by 47 publishers, told the conference that Left publishers should be bringing out books on things like radical gardening and radical DO-It-Yourself. It's a direction that magazines have already taken. The New Left is reading "On Yer Bike", a radical motorbike mag, and Rock Against Racism"s newspaper, "Temporary Hoarding."

– *New Society*
London

Passengers in several lifeboats sank to pass the time.

– Boston Globe

Referring to the Board of Higher Education, Mr. Zuccotti said:

REMEMBER THE NEEDIEST!

– New York Times

It is proposed to use this donation for the purchase of new wenches for our park as the present old ones are in a dilapidated state.

– *Carrolton* (Ohio) *Chronicle*

Americans belong to more than 13,000 associations, including the American Society of Dowsers, The Society of Connoisseurs of Murder and the International Academy of Accredited Twirling Teachers.
The members are described in the 1977 edition of the Encyclopedia of Associations.
There is also a Polish dental association that identifies itself in its by-laws as being for dentists of Polish extraction.

– Washington Post

WASHINGTON, March 10 – Three Federal agencies plan to conduct a joint study of the usefulness of marijuana in preventing nausea in persons who must take a powerful anti-cancer drug.

– New York Times

ERRATUM

The sketch of Mr. Norman Kent on page 1194 of WHO'S WHO IN AMERICA, 35th Edition, contains the erroneous datum of his having been the recipient of the Lenin Peace Prize for 1967 from the U.S.S.R. This item unfortunately was edited into Mr. Kent's sketch through error of an editor who should have inserted it into the sketch of another biographee, which immediately followed that of Mr. Norman Kent on the printer's galley (though not in the book).

Mr. Norman Kent has received no prize, award or recognition from the U.S.S.R., and we apologize to him for this error.

The Editors

With 23½ pints, the two ladies were high players in four tables of duplicate bridge.

- Martinsburg Journal

Nothing gives a greater variety to the appearance of a house than a few undraped widows.

- House and Garden

INTERVIEW BY IRA MILLER, SAN FRANCISCO CHRONICLE, WITH JOE ALTOBELLI, MANAGER OF THE SAN FRANCISCO GIANTS:

MILLER: In the past, Joe, you've treated Lavelle and Moffitt as virtual equals...Is that no longer true?

ALTOBELLI: No, I'm not saying that. The key was a left-hander, their bench was left-handed, and I went with it. What is this, some bleepin' kind of third degree?

MILLER: I'm just asking.

ALTOBELLI: Well, bleep you. As that, son of a b----. Take it for what it's bleepin' worth. What the bleep. Christ. We win the ballgame two-to-one and you're bleepin' giving me the bleeping third degree. Go bleep in your bleepin' hat. What the bleep. You're trying to tell me how to bleepin' manager, is that right?

MILLER: I'm asking a question about why you did that?

ALTOBELLI: Oh, bullspit. Those bleepin' questions are horsebleep. That's what I think of those bleepin' questions.

- Transcript as reported by
The Washington Times

After Governor Baldridge watched the lion perform, he was taken to Main Street and fed twenty-five pounds of raw meat in front of the Fox Theater.

- Idaho Statesman

Clarification

The Wall Street Journal is glad to make clear to those who read our article of May 19, "Drugs Are Preying on the Prep Schools," that the "Stephen P." (a pseudonym for someone whose name is not Stephen) of the Taft School who was identified as having a drug habit is clearly not to be confused with Steven R. P. who has just graduated from Taft this year with the class of 1983 and who has no such history or habit.

Opening ceremonies will be held at noon Tuesday and the dignitaries instead of cutting a ribbon, will cut in half a 10 inch loaf of bread supplied by the Kaufman Banking Co. The bread will be given to a home for the needy.

- Upstate (N.Y.) Business Journal

Through her 40 years in education Mrs. Tew has always had a positive outlook. Even when it comes to discipline.

"You have to love children," she said. "We must have apathy instead of sympathy."

- Dothan Eagle

Mix jello as directed on box. Sit in refrigerator for about a half hour till it starts to gel. Then add cottage cheese and crushed pineapple.

- Jackson (Mo.) Post & Cash Book

Nowadays the death of an entertainment idol seems to have less and less effect on his or her career.

- Publishers Weekly

DETROIT, April 6 (UPI) - A first-degree murder charge against Hayward Brown, accused in the Dec. 27 shootings of two Detroit policemen, was dropped Friday for a lack of bombing and napalming.

- New York Times

Paul F. McPherson, executive vice president, McGraw-Hill Publications Company, has been named "Communicator of the Year..."

In his acceptance remarks, the M-H executive commented to an audience of more than 150 corporate, advertising and media managers on the future of business publications.

"The data base will grow as an information source through the expansion of the selective dissemination concept of knowledge exchange."

- McGraw-Hill News

Most people, unfortunately, think that if you have a problem you must lie on a coach and talk about the past.

- Port Chester (N.Y.) Daily Item

In 1980 you pay $180 of your first 60 days in a hospital, then $45,000 daily for the 61st through 90th days. All the rest is paid for.

- Orlando Sentinel Star

"Our relief pitching was damned good, great," said manager Whitey Herzog, who violated a sacred cow for the second time in a week and got by with it.

- Dallas Morning News

John Sherwood whose farm lies just east of Warnerville Hill road told the The Times-Journal that Charles Ingraham, the mail carrier, spied a bear crossing John's property Friday a short distance above Charles Phelan's farm, stopping at the next house to tell John Snellbaker.

- Cobleskill (N.Y.) Times-Journal

"...if while skiing, you fall and hit your head and are uconscious, even momentarily, you must take yourself off the slopes, and you must see a physician."

- Skiing

After a routine FAA inspection, Munz Airlines has temporarily grounded their fleet. Apparently, service has not been affected.

- Fairbanks Tundra Times

```
N002
RN
R NIX


AP-ADVISORY

    THE SCHEDULED 3 P.M. NEWS CONFERENCE BY THE PEOPLE'S COMMITTEE FOR
STUDENTS TO DISCUSS THE ARREST AND DETENTION OF ALI GHABBAN HAS BEEN
CANCELLED.
    SPOKESWOMAN HELEN HAJE SAYS GHABBAN WILL BE PLACED ON A PAN AM
FLIGHT LEAVING DULLES AIRPORT AT 4 P.M.
    THE A-P WASHINGTON
AP-NX-06-18-83 1502EDT
```

The formal transfer of judicial and law enforcement powers means the U.S. special police force in the Canal Zone will be disbanded and Panamanian police and courts will now arrest and try all U.S. and Panamanian residents of the zone.

- *San Francisco Chronicle*

A woman reported that a man was committing an obscene act in his car. Police investigated and the man explained that he was putting out a fire in his car caused by a cigarette.

- *Providence Journal*
  (McLean, Va.)

I wanted a bunny suit. I just felt like it. Naturally most of the shops were clean out of bunnies, it being the day before Easter, but finally one guy told me he might have one my size if I rushed right down. Which I did. And he did - a white woolly one with floppy pink ears and a dumb round tail. And I wore it right out of the store, got in the car, drove down Hollywood Boulevard...and this amazing thing happened. People began staring at me, and instead of feeling embarrassed, I felt...I don't know...*strengthened*, more confident, healthier.

- David Felton
  Rolling Stone

Florynce Kennedy, a New York feminist attorney, called Uganda President Idi Amin "an outstanding figure" at a Yale Law School conference in New Haven Saturday.
Kennedy said that much of the public criticism of Amin can be traced to the attitude that "if a black person is in charge of a country he isn't really supposed to be in charge." Commenting on the charges that Amin has directed the killings of thousands in his country, she said "Sovereign governments are in the process of killing people all the time." As to the alleged murder of Anglican Bishop Janini Luwum, she said, "The men who died in Vietnam aren't any less dead than Bishop Luwum."

- Washington Post

(STORY IN ITS ENTIRETY)

SACRAMENTO, Calif. (AP) - Can four fake owls scare a flock of starlings away?

Police hit upon the idea of placing some fake owls in the trees by the police building because birds droppings were fouling vehicles parked underneath. Owls, someone told them, were the natural enemies of starlings.

A work crew, however, placed the owls in the wrong trees. But it was all right.

— Pasco-Kennewick-Richland (Wash.) Tri-City Herald

DEAR HELOISE:

When freezing vegetables, I use white nylon net, cut in yard squares.

I place the vegetables in the center of the net (doubled or tripled, if necessary) and tie up the four corners.

After dropping the bag of vegetables into the boiling
doors. Remove poisons, including dirty ashtrays, peeling paint, etc. Cover electrical outlets.

— Red Bank (N.J.) Daily Register

HIS BILL WOULD REQUIRE THAT ALL ABORTIONS BE PERFORMED BY

REPUBLICANS AND THAT THE OPERATIONS BE DONE IN LICENSED HOSPITALS

AFTER THE 12TH WEEK.

— Associated Press Radio Wire

Hardly a day goes by that you can't hear an announcer say something like this, "We'll be back at the 20th Olympiad after this message." An Olympiad is a period of time, the four years from one Olympics to the next.

— Sports Section New York Times, Sept. 10, 1972

Gathered in the name of peace and sportsmanship, the 20th Olympiad of modern times will disperse tomorrow under the shadow of an act of international terrorism.

— Week in Review New York Times. Sept. 10, 1972

WASHINGTON (AP) - One of the latest of the Watergate books claims that Richard M. Nixon's predecessors committed "numerous political excesses, some of which make Watergate look like penny-ante stuff."

Victor Lasky writes in "It Didn't Start With Watergate," that the affair "has been blown up out of all proportions to the realities, becoming a veritable teapot in a tempest."

— Dallas Morning News

"We really have to deal with all sorts of things," said Anne. "The trouble that we have with how to spell 'Bermudian' is really a problem.

"That little 'i' causes so much trouble. The worst offenders are Lloyd's Shipping Register, who always spell 'Bermudian' as 'Bermudian.'

"I rang them up once to tell them about this and they said, 'Well, you might spell it Bermudian but to us it's Bermudian.'

"That was the end of that," she said.

— Hamilton (Bermuda) Mid-Ocean News

The White House advisers to Mr. Nixon thought that the scientists were using science as a sledgehammer to grind their political axes.

- Washington Post

At the next traffic light, the Latins again spotted their colleague, this time slouched in his seat, motionless, with his chin propped on his elbow.

- New York Times

Rhodesian Premier Ian Smith's son Alex says his father is prepared to reign if it would help settle the Rhodesian problem.

- Washington Star

WASHINGTON (AP) - Former Mice President Spiro T. Egnew drew applause when he arrived at a local sports arena for a concert by singer Frank Sinatra.

- Richmond News Leader

By the time most students reach age 17, their mastery has improved markedly. More than half of the 17-year-olds display a "sound grasp of the bsics of written language." except for spelling and word choice. Only 15 per cent show a werious lack of ability in those basics.

- Spokane Spokesman

Mikhelson said in an interview this month archeologists might have been useable for such a project if they had not been put into strong formaldehyde preservative solutions by their discoverers.

- Michigan Daily

We strongly support the honey industry be given preference over the welfare of the Florida bear.

- FloridAgriculture

A CORRECTION

It was erroneously reported in last week's MAILeader that the cost of spraying ten caterpillars in Valley Stream would be $31,000. The figure should have read $3,100.

- Valley Stream (N.Y.)
MAILeader

A reception was held at the Mount Stephen Club where Mr. Will played for dancing. The couple later left for a motor trip amid confetti and tiny snowballs travelling in casual clothes.

- Montreal Gazette

The couple gets their antiques through a buyer in Los Gatos who has a broker in England and accepts antiques on consignment from local persons in good condition

- Felton (Ca.) Valley Press

Since she's back in New York, she finds that shopping is more convenient, she can see the latest art and dance shows, greet the kids when they come home from school, have dinner at a number of fine restaurants and go to the theater - all in one day.

- New York Times

Mary Carroll, formerly public relations director with the Dominican Republic Tourist Information Center, has been named public relations manager of the Western Hemisphere.

- Travel Weekly

There was an officer on patrol after midnight on the night of May 27. He was involved in an arrest at 1 a.m. and assisting a Framingham trooper on Rte. 9 in a holdup for the rest of the night.

- Boston Globe

(WASHINGTON) -- SECRETARY OF STATE ROGERS SAID TODAY THERE IS A GOOD POSSIBILITY THE CEASE-FIRE WILL BECOME EFFECTIVE IN WASHINGTON.

- Associated Press

The command said the MiGs jets fired two air-to-air missiles at the American planes during the brief dogfight and that the Phantoms fired one missile at the MiGs.

The provisional wing of the illegal Irish Republican Army (IRA) claimed responsibility for the blast, which also smashed the front of a Woolworth's store.

- Rockford *Morning Star*

If Leonardo da Vinci had been born a female the ceiling of the Sistine Chapel might never have been painted.

- Philadelphia Welcomat

"I can contribute to Taylor government with new ideas and leadership backed with common sense, courtesy and an open mind. Your support and vote for Ted Krebs, City Commission April 2, 1977 will be most sincerely appreciated."

The monetary unit of the Mongolian People's Republic is the "tughrik."

- Taylor (Texas) *Daily Press*

The first was the deputy secretary of state, regarded by the White House inner circle as a man of loyalty and capability, qualities whose importance to a White House cannot be underestimated.

- Martin Schram,
- Philadelphia Inquirer

"If Beale Street could talk," as the song goes, it would tell a fantastic tale of New Orleans.

- The Journal of the American Medical Association

If this is true, the results of the week's events will be more favorable to democratic forces inside and outside Ecuador than had been feared.

- New York Times

TV LISTINGS:

7:00
Political (4): Daniel J. Evans for Governor. Paid political broadcast. (Local preemption of To Tell The Truth.)

- Seattle *Times*

KILL 11-1

BULLETIN KILL

EDITORS:

KILL FLYNN NEW YORK 299A. FLYNN IS NOT DEAD.

UPI NEW YORK

   UPI 11-01 09:14 PES

Named Great Adventure, the amusement complex is expected to attack two million visitors during its first year of operations.

   - Trenton *Times*

The two-horned white rhinoceros of Southeast Asia, believed to be on the edge of extinction, is now thriving in the jungles of northern Malaysia, according to Harold Stephens, an American free-lance reporter who together with some Malaysians found rhino wallows in a northern national park. The exact location was not revealed because the discoverers fear that poachers would find the rhinos and wipe them out for their horns, which are highly prized in oriental medicines.

   The evidence found included recently stripped tires, which are the exclusive and unique diet of the big animals.

   - *World Envirnoment Report*

Overhead new Sabre jets, given to Spain by the United States, whistled low over the trees...General Franco himself could be seen on the reviewing stand following the fighters as they swept out of sight.

   - New York Times

CORRECTION

The News apologizes for the error that appeared in last week's ad for P.C. Kellam, Jr.
   The ad read "A Man who will work against higher education." It should have read..."against higher taxes."

   - *Accomac (Va.)
   Eastern Shore Press*

But most serious of all is the problem of safety. Both cyclists and motorists live in fear of collisions, particularly after dark when the light is bad.

   - *The Economist*

Mon., Feb. 14 - In the Beverly Hills Hotel, White Female suspect hit victim and fled with same.

   - *Police Blotter,
   Beverly Hills Courier*

He said the plane was named after his mother, Enola Gay Tibbets, "cause I knew this plane would go down in history and I wanted to name it for my mother, who was the only one to encourage me to fly."

   - Section B, p.12

Before coming to Tuscon, all four met and talked at length with Tibbets. The captain was 29 when he led his crew over Japan. The Enola Gay was named for his mother who had always discouraged her son from pursuing flying.

   Section I, p. 1

(Both stories are from the same day's edition of the *Arizona Daily Star*.)

The central bank has been working on redefinitions of money supply measures that it hopes will be "more meaningful for economic interpretation." The new definitions are to be announced next yesterday.

- San Francisco Chronicle

Twentieth Century-Fox's sports head, Shelly Saltman, will spend a month on the road between Hawaii and the mainland, producing shows on tennis and gymnastics. That's not bad traveling.

- Hank Grant,

San Francisco Chronicle

The party is debt-free due to the efforts of Governors Hoff and Salmon. As a result of the Muskie fundraiser held in November and other fundraising efforts we now have approximately $7,000 in the party's coiffure.

- Vermont Democratic Newsletter

A recipe for marjolaine in The Living Section on Wednesday omitted an ingredient for the pastry cream. The recipe should have included two

- New York Times

Andrews is awaiting a court decision in the case, but also plans to petition city officials to change a local ordnance that says trains may move slowly as long as they are going in one direction.

- Portland (Me.) Press Herald

Seventy-one bishops of the United Methodist Church from the United States and several foreign countries will be fathering in Des Moines for the biennial meeting of the Council of Bishops of United Methodists.

Newton, Ia., *Daily News*

Sitting in a leather arm chair in his office, Kline considered the key attributes of a successful businessman. "Integrity, voracity, and spirituality," he almost snapped out.

- Norfolk Virginian-Pilot

WASHINGTON (UPI) - President Carter yesterday nominated Wisconsin Gov. Patrick Lucey to be ambassador to Mexico, and formally announced he was naming former Senate Democratic leader Mike Mansfield as ambassador to Japan and Yale and Yale president Kingman Brewster to Britain.

- Van Nuys Valley News

You remember Liddy. He's the one guy in the Nixon White House mess who refused to talk about it. Loyalty, dedication were a couple of adjectives that added to his mystique.

Editorial,
Syracuse Herald-Journal

According to the minutes of the May 7, 1980 meeting of the hospital's Department of Pediatrics, "It was unanimously agreed that the Nurse Midwifery Protocol would not be accepted or approved, nor would it be reviewed by the Pediatric Department until a newborn physician is recruited as a sole back-up for the Nurse Midwifery Practice.

- Nashville Tennessean

Sgt. Joseph Panogia attributed the decline to the arrest and subsequent incarnation of a few people in the area.

Saddle Brook (N.J.) *News Dispatch*

(Story in its Entirety)

DRAGONFLIES HARMLESS

Dragonflies are harmless.

- Arkansas Gazette

But officials said rain forced a cancellation, even though there was no rain during those hours.

- AP report,
Cleveland *Plain Dealer*,
Sept. 11, 1972

Olympic officials were saved from the embarassment of a ceremony boycott by the American basketball team when a deluge washed out the medal presentation ceremony.

- UPI report,
Cleveland *Press*,
Sept. 11, 1972

Because of intermarriage, her husband had only one great-grandfather, though most people of course have eight.

- 𝔚𝔞𝔰𝔥𝔦𝔫𝔤𝔱𝔬𝔫 𝔓𝔬𝔰𝔱

Perhaps the ultimate in mistakes in a booklet that purports to give facts about Stamford is that the word "Stamford" itself appears incorrectly twice. It comes out "Stamford." Oy!

- *Stamford Advocate*

(DENVER) -- ONE-HUNDRED AND 30 MILES NORTHEAST OF DENVER TODAY

THE HIJACKER OF AN AIRWEST JETLINER IS BELIEVED TO HAVE BAILED OUT

-- COMING DOWN ON A FARM IN THE GRASSY PLAINS AREA SEVEN MILES

NORTHEAST OF AKRON, OHIO.

- AP Radio Wire

Dieruff is back with a third clock. Called Talk Time, it will actually speak the correct time. Chip components enable the device to operate using only 10 sounds, one for each number between zero and nine.
At 10:32, for example, the clock would say "one-zero-five-two."

- *Montreal Gazette*

By Marilyn Goldstein

LA Times Slug

- Salem (Ore.)
Capital Journal

Since opening the class in Winamac I have given 5-20 pound awards. I have two members who have almost 20 pounds off. I have one member who has almost 50 pounds off. And one who has lost all her weight and now is on our maintenance program.

"Social Scene"
- Pulaski County (Ind.) *Press*

This is the time of the year if anybody quotes Joyce Kilmer's poem (Trees," I just shake my head and say, "That poetess hasn't had a rake in her hands and tried to keep ahead of having her total lawn iced with a thick carpet of leaves."

— Alice Wessels Burlingame,
Birmingham (Mich.) *Eccentric*

PEPIN DIES

Pepin, king of the Franks and father of Charlemagne, died in 768.

— *Champaign-Urbana News-Gazette*

An average of forty German youths are enlisted each day. About forty others are rejected, usually on grounds of physical fitness.

— New York Times

I have been raising the question for some years, but is is like the tree that falls in the dessert: Nobody hears it.

— *Fort Collins Coloradoan*

The Soviet shoe industry produced about three shoes for each person.

— New York Times

The statement commented on the report of a stud mission sent to Indochina by Sen. Edward M. Kennedy, D-Mass., chairman of the Senate Judiciary subcommittee on refugees.

— Associated Press

Pity the poor Pratt City Commission. On one side there are vandals who destroy city property, close the swimming pool, and create general havoc.
On the other side are groups of citizens urging for renewed efforts to beautify the rose garden. The trouble is, the Commission wants to help both of these worthwhile causes, but has the money to do neither.

— *Pratt* (Kans.) *Tribune*

Mrs. Gandhi must receive a stream of ordinary Indians, most of them with grievances, every morning at her official residence.
But at No. 12 Willingdon Crescent, her former home, her son holds court with close associates, political workers and naked self-seekers.

— *Kuwait Times*

Equitable Equipment Co. of New Orleans, shipbuilder, has changed its name to Equitable Shipyards, Inc. A wholly owned subsidiary of Trinity Industries, Equitable (founded in 1921) is one of the world's largest medium-sized shipbuilding concerns.

— *New Orleans Times-Picayune*

President Carter said the United States is not considering new military measures to free the hostages, but his press secretary, Jody Powell, explained that Carter meant no military measures are being considered.

— *Newsday*

The Hubble Constant - a speed to distance ratio used to calculate how rapidly the universe is expanding - is twice as big as most scientists thought, according to the latest theory. This means the universe is nine billion years old, not eighteen billion years old, and is only half the size previously thought.

A small error can result in a 20 percent adjusted gross income ceiling on a charitable remainder deduction (instead of a 50 percent or 30 percent ceiling), according to a recent revenue ruling.

- New York Journal

Egypt will be allowed by the U.S. government to buy F-15s and F-16s thus achieving symbolic equality with Israel. Because of budget considerations, however, Egypt will buy only the F-16s, which cost $20 millions each, whereas the other plane costs $20 millions each.

- Newburyport (Mass.)
Daily News

Wednesday morning, Lee's oldest son Mike signed a national letter of intent with Indiana University to play football for the Hoosiers in the family kitchen at 2838 Ashland Dr. in West Lafayette.

- Lafayette (Ind.)
Journal & Courier

RHODE ISLAND SENATOR JOHN PASTORE SAYS THE NAVY HAS ALMOST COMPLETELY WIPED OUT MASSACHUSETTS AND RHODE ISLAND.

- AP New England Radio Wire

As for getting her money's worth from Heartwood, Diane believes she did. "I knew zero when I went there and now I know one-hundred percent more. I've had my eyes opened."

- Media (Pa.) Town Talk

Under Taiwan's martial law proceedings, defendants are not regarded as innocent unless proved guilty.

- New York Times

Facilities include two tennis courts, an 18-hole swimming pool and a health club.

- San Francisco Examiner

CORRECTION

In Saturday's Enterprise an article on the Church of Jesus Christ of Latter-Day Saints - the Mormons - incorrectly said that 1.06 million members of the church live in Utah, "a state in which 70 percent take LSD."

The article should have read "a state which is 70 percent LDS (Latter-Day Saints)."

- Brockton
Enterprise

8:05 p.m. - WGMS (570) & WGMS-FM (103.5). WGMS Live. Baritone William Parker and pianist Jeffrey Goldberg perform music by Lieder and Chanson.

- Washington Post

Joining Wallace on stage were new School Committeewoman Elvira Pixie Palladino and Boston City Councilman Albert (Dapper) O'Neil, both active opponents of court-ordered busing and Wallace's wife Cornelia.

- Boston Globe

Mrs. Ethel Saling of La Grande returned home last Thursday after spending two weeks in Reno visiting her son, Jim, and family. While there, her grandson James D. Saling was married in the Catholic Church with a reception following. After she returned home a call was received announcing that she was a grandmother.

- Eastern Oregon Review

The campaign for the Oct. 3 elections is being fought the width and the breath of the city.

- New York Times

Simon Gray's dogs were friendly beyond belief, and he himself offered a welcome of a lime-juice cordiality - cool, non-fizzy, tangy but not sour. When I spilled my drink on the Persian Rug, he produced a cloth with Hench-like deftness and politesse - "I believe white wine is good for the carpet." His own foot later trod a centimetre away from the luckless glass, but my warning was unnecessary. His leg was perfectly still and aware; no way would it ever have moved that fatal fraction.

- Janet Watts,
The Guardian

Montreal police don't hesitate to use whatever laws, regulations or persuasion they feel they need to control morality in the city and prevent it from getting a foothold in any one part of the city.

- Toronto Globe & Mail

INTERVIEW WITH THE DUKE OF NORFOLK

THE DUKE: Sit down and have a drink. Do you smoke? Curious, all the cigarette boxes have diappeared. (Rings bell: butler appears.) Rawlings, have we been burgled?
RAWLINGS: Not that I am aware of, your grace.
THE DUKE: All the silver has been removed.
RAWLINGS: It is being cleaned, your Grace.
THE DUKE: That's much more satisfactory.
His humor had three qualities: it was dry, sardonic and laconically expressed. He was a master of meiosis. A great deal of his style is to be found in Mark Twain.

- Kenneth Harris
The Observer

Once again, the dairy farmer was literally milked almost dry.

- Wall Street Journal

Cleve Backster, the patron of emotion in plants (on the basis of one unduplicated test), now reports finding evidence of feelin yogurt. He said he had found a trace of jealousy (or pleasedness) between one yogurt container and the next, which had been fed some milk.

- New York Times

DOCTORS AT NEW YORK HOSPITAL SAY A BABY GIRL WEIGHING JUST

A LITTLE MORE THAN A POUND AND A HALF IS HOLDING OUT UNDER

SPECIAL CARE DESPITE THE FACT SHE WAS BORN 15 MONTHS PREMATURELY.

— UPI RADIO WIRE

At one point, Colby seemed to be suggesting that the CIA's production, in collaboration with the Army, of cultures other agencies are trying to obliterate, like brucellosis and TV, for instance, had been motivated by humanitarian concerns.

— *Chicago Tribune*

Q — I ax a widow with $110,000, all invested in one municipal bond issue because of the tax exemption. But I am worried about it.

— *Tarrytown Daily News*

OWNERS OF ALL DOGS IN THE

CITY OF METROPOLIS ARE REQUIRED

TO BE ON A CHAIN OR IN A FENCED

IN AREA.

— Metropolis (Ill.) *Planet*

And during the current fiscal year, Kinney plans to increase the number of uninformed sergeants by 14, making a total of 42.

— Sacremento *Bee*

He received his graduate degree in unclear physics.

— Moline *Daily Dispatch*

Z-I-I-I-P!

PULASKI, Va. July 8 (UPI)— Gov. Charles S. Robb pulled down the zipper and walked through the fly of a giant pair of blue jeans today to open the new Lee Co. plant here.

— *Washington Post*

CORRECTION

The New York Times reported Jan. 11 that Senator Henry M. Jackson, Democrat of Washington, had said he favored cutting the oil depletion allowance to 27½ per cent from the 28 per cent level set by Congress in 1969.

— *New York Times*, Jan. 22, 1973

CORRECTION

The New York Times reported Jan. 11 that Senator Henry M. Jackson, Democrat of Washington, had said he favored returning the oil depletion allowance to 27½ per cent from the 22 per cent level voted by Congress in 1969.

— *New York Times*, Jan. 24, 1973

William Andrews returned home yesterday from the hospital, where his left leg was placed in a cast following a fracture of the right ankle.

- *Malone (N.Y.) Telegram*

One can peek in most any evening on this home-loving young actress and find her cuddled up in an easy chair with a good boob before a crackling fire.

- *Hollywood Citizen-News*

MIAMI, Fla.-Albert Cox, embezzler, endorsed checks for $90,299.77 last year. For nine months he played the daily double, sipped dry martinis, dallied with expensive prostitutes, flew first class city to city, and spent the rest foolishly.

- 𝕭𝖔𝖘𝖙𝖔𝖓 𝕰𝖛𝖊𝖓𝖎𝖓𝖌 𝕲𝖑𝖔𝖇𝖊

CORRECTIONS

The title of Henry A. Kissinger's previous book, reported in The Times on Friday as "A World Destroyed," is "A World Restored: Castlereagh, Metternich and the Restoration of Peace, 1812-1822."

- 𝕹𝖊𝖜 𝖄𝖔𝖗𝖐 𝕿𝖎𝖒𝖊𝖘

Electronics is taught by Mr. Finis Walker. This course is mainly a program designed to enable students to become inept in repairing TVs, radios and other electronical equipment.

- *Easton (Md.) Star-Democrat*

To acquaint employees with Mansfield Tire's group of general foremen, we will try to report the personal histories of these important clogs in our plant machinery.

- *Tire Topics*

(Introduction to mid-newscast commercial)

"More on that coming back, I'll be up in a moment."

- Robert MacNeil, NBC News

CHICAGO (AP) - A Circuit Court of Appeals has affirmed a federal court order that requires U.S. Steel Corp. to drastically reduce by July 1 the discharge of politicians from its Gary Works into Lake Michigan.

- *Houston Post*

Gene Autry is better after being kicked by a horse.

- *Omaha Sunday World-Herald*

Fog and smog rolled over Los Angeles today, closing two airports and slowing snails to a traffic pace.

- *Los Angeles News*

SAFER NITRO: Sweden's AB Bofors had developed a new method of manufacturing and shipping nitroglycerine powder in a water suspension. It almost entirely eliminates the risky process once used in some plants which no longer exist.

- *Oakland Tribune*

Rep. Bill Heatly, D-Paducah, said the present system is working well and should not be left as it is.

- San Angelo (Texas) *Times*

The rules for doing this - for escaping from quicksand fix, should you find yourself in one - are simple. The basic rule is, don't panic. That's the advice of the late quicksand expert, Gerard H. Matthes of the United States Geological Survey.

-Boston Globe

POLICE BLOTTER:

VANDALISM

Ball glued to pool table - at Senior Citizen Center, reported at 3:45 p.m. Friday by Frank Mullen, no estimate of damage.

- Mason City-Clear Lake
(Iowa) Globe-Gazette

TOKYO (AP) - Japan's first experimental stationary satellite continued to function normally and appeared to have shifted to a circular orbit from an eliptical orbit Saturday afternoon, the National Space Development Agency said.

Her lawyers, in the meantime, were given until 2 p.m. Monday to appeal.

- Staten Island Advance

(Story in its Entirety)

St. Kitts, West Indies (UPI) - The man shelled a last peanut, rose, forgetting to put on one shoe, raised his umbrella and walked out the front door, noticing as he did that the dog had dug a hole there.

All seemingly innocent actions. But any expert in West Indies superstitions could have forecast that all hell was about to break loose in that man's life.

- Santa Fe New Mexican

In some of the 152 cases, "agency expertise" was manifested in the ability to correct errors so minute they were obviously typographical.

- New Jersey
Law Journal

Winds up to 45 mph toppled a one-ton tree onto a tent at a county fair in Topsfield, Mass. No injuries were reported among 125 people watching a goat-judging show but two goats fainted, officials said. The goats were revived by mouth-to-mouth resuscitation.

- Rocky Mountain News

August 2 - All programs and activities must be accessible physically to the handicapped except where structural changes are required. A school could comply, for example, by moving classes from one floor to another, putting in wheelchair ramps, or providing certain auxiliary aids like interpreters for the dead.

- Seattle Post-Intelligencer

In addition, there is the persistent question of incorporation. Orinda residents have voted incorporation down poration. Orinda residents have voted incorporation down poration. Orinda residents have voted incorporation down poration. Orinda residents have down incorporation down each time it has reached the ballot, but will this go on indefinitely?

- *Orinda* (Calif.) *Sun*

The social affair is being planned as a retribution to the hospitality offered recently to the British ladies, at the home of Mrs. Wendy Luers, wife of the American Ambassador.

- *Caracas Daily Journal*

A new ruling by the Federal Reserve permits theft institutions to pay rate in the certificates $1\frac{1}{2}$ below the current yield on $2\frac{1}{2}$ year Treasury securities.

- *Pasco (Wash.)*
  Tri-City Herald

O'Meara has missed several council meetings since the beginning of the year.
He has appeared at those he attended.

- *Hartford Courant*

Then, just for kicks, John Kazian walks along the top wing at speeds approaching 200 miles an hour.

- Milwaukee *Sentinel*

Einstein said, "A clock in motion keeps time more slowly than one that is moving."

- *San Francisco Chronicle*

Of Sunday's drama, Ryan's closet friend, coach Jimmie Reese, 70, said, "I'm going to go home and faint."

- 𝕷𝖔𝖘 𝕬𝖓𝖌𝖊𝖑𝖊𝖘 𝕿𝖎𝖒𝖊𝖘

Shakespeare didn't have public television in mind when he warned about the ideas of March.

- *Television/Radio Age*

SENATOR GEORGE MCGOVERN OF SOUTH DAKOTA, ALSO CAMPAIGNING

FOR THE PRIMARY, APPEALED FOR THE VOTES OF BLUE-COLORED

WORKERS IN MILWAUKEE.

- AP Radio Wire

The Tangerine Bowl-bound Gators have lost three in a row to Florida State and reportedly have devoted five minutes a day this week to "hate Florida State."
"We hate them. Everyone hates them. We have to show 'em on the field. Like the good book says, 'Do unto others as they do unto you,' junior fullback Calvin Davis said.

- 𝖂𝖆𝖘𝖍𝖎𝖓𝖌𝖙𝖔𝖓 𝕻𝖔𝖘𝖙

Police Officer Bill Avery relied on intuitive judgment when he exposed himself to an armed suspect who had abducted two children. The gamble paid off when the man surrendered.

- *Arlington Citizen Journal*

There was a slight drop in the number of marriage licenses applied for in Ashtabula County in 1976, compared to the previous year, but the number of marriages ending in divorce or disillusion subsided significantly.

— *Ashtabula Star-Beacon*

Steele said investigations of homosexual ring operating in Dallas had proved fruitless until a young man tipped police on the Cole Avenue organization Tuesday.

— Dallas *Times Herald*

FONTANA, Calif., Feb. 15 (AP) - A man shot his estranged wife to death in a bar on Valentine's Day during a spat over an Indian head penny, police said.

— Associated Press report in the 𝔚𝔞𝔰𝔥𝔦𝔫𝔤𝔱𝔬𝔫 ℘𝔬𝔰𝔱

Business loans soared by $1.36 billion in the latest reporting week despite the Carter administration's participation in the Moscow Games. Page 5.

— Daily Index 𝔑𝔢𝔴 𝔜𝔬𝔯𝔨 𝔗𝔦𝔪𝔢𝔰

TV Listing:

"THE BOMBING OF HAIPHONG." 8:30 p.m. (4) (Special) NBC News correspondent Edwin Newman hosts this hour-long program on the Haiphong bombing. The report includes appearances by Secretary of State Rogers and Secretary of Defense Laird before the Senate Foreign Relations Committee. (Preempts the previously scheduled "Thou Shalt Not Kill.")

— 𝔏𝔬𝔰 𝔄𝔫𝔤𝔢𝔩𝔢𝔰 𝔗𝔦𝔪𝔢𝔰

Cambridge residents celebrated the saving of a life yesterday by holding a block party during which they discussed how to prevent similar occurrences in the future.

— 𝔅𝔬𝔰𝔱𝔬𝔫 𝔊𝔩𝔬𝔟𝔢

"We've got talent here, but we are obviously need some shoring up in several positions depth-wise," he said. "This year we have to do a lot of weeding out and see what cream comes to the top."

— *Spokane Statesman-Review*

Dr. Nigrelli, and his wife, Maragret, who live at 11 West 183rd Street, the Bronx, is a native of Pittston, Pa.

— 𝔑𝔢𝔴 𝔜𝔬𝔯𝔨 𝔗𝔦𝔪𝔢𝔰

(Story in its Entirety)

Atari chairman resigns

SUNNYVALE, Calif. (KNT) — Raymond E. Kassar, who led Atari Inc. of Sunnyvale from sales of $200 million to $2 billion in five years, resigned as chairman and chief executive, effective today.

After four days of negotiations, Atari has hired James J. Morgan, the 41-year-old executive vice president of marketing at Philip Morris U.S.A., to replace him.

Although Morgan has excelled at selling Marlboro, Parliament and Virginia Slims cigarettes, he has no experience in the video game or computer business. Like John Sculley.

— *Moline Daily Dispatch*

Take one sick beer business. Stir in a dash of bitters and a soupcon of grenadine. Add generous portions of malt liquor and ale. Season with a heap of chutney. Garnish with a fistful of vitamins and assorted nuts. Age it well, and prune it judiciously. Then top it with a popular chocolate-flavored drink.

— Resa W. King, *The New Englander*

SAINT THOMAS' CHURCH

Huron Street just south of Bloor
between Spadina & St. George subways

SUNDAY MORNING EUCHARISTS

8:00 9:30 (Contemporary)
11:00 (Solemn)
7:00 p.m. Solemn heathen Song &
Devotions

- *Toronto Globe & Mail*

During the height of the annual summer
spawning runs, Rollie Ostermick photo-
graphed a brown bear wallowing for salmon in a secluded Alaskan stream with a
Nikkormat camera and 300mm lens.

- *National Wildlife*

Chinese Cuisine/Looks Rank with Flavor.

- Photo Caption,
Minneapolis Tribune

Some have accused the New Yorker of
a stilted style, such as its frequent use
of the third person "we" in its reporting
on current events.

- *Detroit News*

Former Mafia chieftain Vincent (Big Vin-
nie) Teresa, being deported from Australia, slipped away from a San Francisco-
bound airliner during a refueling stop in
Hawaii. Teresa, who was given a new
identity by the FBI after turning informer,
said before he left Australia, "I know what
the Mafia can do to a man who has crossed
them. One day you wake up and find
Archbishop Makarios, leader of the Greek
Cypriots and president of Cyprus, met
Thursday with special U.S. envoy Clark
Clifford, who was sent to Cyprus by
President Carter to help mediate the Cyprus dispute with Turkey. Makarios
called the visit "very useful and construc-
tive."

- *Chicago Daily News*

Baron, 51, a former Illinois resident,
was accused of wire and mail fraud and
of understanding his gross income on a
1974 federal income tax return.

- 𝔚𝔞𝔰𝔥𝔦𝔫𝔤𝔱𝔬𝔫 𝔓𝔬𝔰𝔱

Dr. Joseph Fondacaro, associate
professor; Department of Physio-
logy; College of Medicine, UC, will
present a seminar in Natural Science
525 at noon. The topic is *Relation-
ships between Bile Acids and Lipid
Acids within the Small Intestine.*
Everyone is encouraged to attend.
Feel free to bring your lunch.

- *The Northerner,
Northern Kentucky
University*

SAVE ON WATER

For hand laundering, put a stopper in
the washtub for both washing and rinsing,
and don't let the water run.

- *Little Rock Gazette*

A hand grenade was discovered and later
successfully detonated at McDonald's Restaurant late Friday night,
The device, according to Kinston police
reports, turned out to be a dud.

- *Kinston (N.C.)
Daily Free Press*

*(HEADLINE AND STORY
IN THEIR ENTIRETIES)*

PROUST DIED IN 1922

Novelist Marcel Proust died in 1922.

- *Madison (Wis.) City Lights*

A New Zealand tourist whose two two-headed children were climbing up the beams of "Ik Ook" (Dutch for "Me Too") contemplated it with a bemused air.

— New York Times

LAIRD SAID THE COUNTRY, IN HIS WORDS, "CANNOT AFFORD TO BE DISTRACTED" FROM SUCH ISSUES AS HEALTH CARE, THE ECONOMY, ECOLOGY AND TEXAS.

— Associated Press

WASHINGTON, Oct. 15 (AP) — President Nixon issued an executive order today to permit all of the Federal agencies and offices to start using a colorful emblem publicizing the 200th anniversary of the nation's foundering.

— New York Times

Q — I am curious about the origin of the names of two fruits - grapefruits, which do not resemble grapes, and pineapples, which do not look like apples. Do you know the answer?

A — Grapefruits are so named because the fruit resembles large pine cones, which contain pine nuts.

— Fayetteville (N.C.) Times

A 48-page color comprehensive forms catalog containing detailed descriptions and practical helpful hints on how to sue Eimicke Personnel Forms is available from V. W. Eimicke Associates, Inc. Bronxville, N.Y.

— Administrative Management

As the election results became more decisive, the crowds at Mrs, Gandhi's home here grew. Enterprising flower merchants set up stands on her street selling the garlands that the faithful bring her and to which she is allergic.

— Cleveland Plain Dealer

Statewide, students performed extremely poor on the writing section of the exam.

— New Orleans Times Picayune

She also is an experienced public accountant, having worked for Peat, Marwick, Mitchell & Co. in Honolulu from 1973 and for Coopers & Lybrand in New York from 1973 to 1975.

— American Banker

Equally as talented were the four young men backing the vocalists, Mike Allsup, guitar; Jimmy Greenspoon, keyboards; Joel Schermie, bass; and Floyd Sneed, drugs.

— Rocky Mountain News

The AFSC began by reconstruction work in World War I and fed the needy of all views after the Russian Revolution, headed by future President Herbert Hoover,

— Washington Post

About talk of massive power losses this summer: Discount scare stories that have shown up in the sensational tabloids - the fear is being hypoed.

Major brownouts are not expected as of now, not in the Eastern U.S. or anywhere else, for that matter - nothing like the June 1967 blackout. The power companies have plenty of juice, will move it around as necessary to prevent anything but mild, sporadic brownouts on the hottest summer days.

- *U.S. News Washington Letter*

(STORY IN ITS ENTIRETY)

SACRAMENTO (AP) - Gov. Edmund Brown, Jr. has approved a $75,000 California share of the Tahoe Regional Planning Commission budget for 1977-78 - with a string attached.

- *Palo Alto Times*

The macadamia was named for Dr. John MacAdam, an enthusiastic scientist who promoted the nut in its native Australia, and was dubbed "the perfect nut" by Luther Burbank.

- Los Angeles *Herald Examiner*

Maidenhead, England - (AP) - Thieves recently stole two large pumpkins from a garden here.

However, they ignored an even larger pumpkin because, says a policeman.

- *Seattle Post-Intelligencer*

Due to an oversight the change of date of our craft fair was not announced. It was held earlier but the original date was announced on the later date also.

We are very sorry for any inconvenience we may have caused to anyone.

BROWNVILLE GEN. HIS. SOC.

- *Watertown Daily Times*

MUSH FROM THE WIMP

(*Boston Globe* editorial title commenting on speech by President Carter outlining steps to curb inflation)

March 15, 1980

AN APOLOGY

The first editions of last Saturday's Globe carried a headline on the lead editorial that was inappropriate and not intended for publication. In later editions the editorial, which supported President Carter's new initiatives on the economy, was titled, "All must share the burden."

- 𝕭𝖔𝖘𝖙𝖔𝖓 𝕲𝖑𝖔𝖇𝖊
March 18, 1980

HOROSCOPE:

Libra (Sept. 23-Oct.22) - You do well to shape erry wilder 10-1 P2 your course around existing materials; otherwise, frustrations result.

- *Grand Rapids Press*

MILFORD - Bring on the tax forms - there are volunteer counselors at Milford public library to help senior citizens fill them out.

The International Revenue Service-trained volunteers will start their sting Feb. 5 and be at the library from 10 a.m. until 3 p.m. every Tuesday until April 8.

- *Dover Delaware State News*

(Photo Caption)

During the reception in the Free Library, Mrs. E. Shirley Turner (left) talks with Mr. and Mrs. Joseph S. Rambo. Mrs. Turner, here from Virginia, is a cousin of Princess Grace. Mr. and Mrs. Rambo are friends.

- 𝕻𝖍𝖎𝖑𝖆𝖉𝖊𝖑𝖕𝖍𝖎𝖆 𝕴𝖓𝖖𝖚𝖎𝖗𝖊𝖗

Perhaps the French language will always be the same, even if the prestigious Academie Francaise has broken a 345-year tradition. The academy, dedicated to guarding the purity of the French language, has agreed and voted to membership in the 40 "immortals" to 76-year-old Belgian-born novelist Marguerite Yourcenar. Miss Yourcenar has dual French-U.S. citizenship and is the only American other than Julien Green accepted into the esteemed group. She took the coup de grace of her career in stride.

- Atlanta Journal

BOISE, IDAHO (AP) - A DELAY IN DECIDING WHETHER STATE EMPLOYES WOULD BE MADE MONTHLY, TWICE A MONTH OR EVERY TWO WEEKS WAS CRITICIZED TODAY...

- Associated Press

"ELEPHANT MAN" CHANGE

Bernard Pomerance's "The Elephant Man" will now open at the Playhouse in Wilmington on Oct. 20 instead of at the Forrest in Philadelphia. The play will begin a four-week run at the Forrest on Oct. 20.

- Philadelphia Bulletin

(SACRAMENTO) -- STATE SENATOR ANTHONY BEILENSON INTRODUCED TWO "CONSUMER INTEREST" BILLS IN THE LEGISLATURE YESTERDAY. ONE MEASURE WOULD REQUIRE RESTROOMS TO POST A SIGN IF THEY SERVE OLEOMARGARINE.

- UPI Radio Wire

In an effort to reach as many of my constituents as possible, throughout the year I have been holding Town Hall Meetings. These sessions provide an opportunity for me to learn some of the issues that are on my mind.

- Newsletter of U.S.
Representative
Charles P. Rangel

By the time the Vatican's highly skilled conservators finish their restoration, the damage wrought on the "Pieta" yesterday will be discernible only to the most educated eye examining Michelangelo's masterpeice at very close range.

- Page 2,
New York *News*
May 22, 1972

Francesco Vacchini, head of the basilica's technical office, told reporters that the statue "will never be the same again." He said that although the broken parts could be glued back in, the cracks would always remain visible.

- Page 35.
New York *News*
May 22, 1972

"The reason nothing has been done is because no one has made any effort to do anything about it," said one transportation official.

- 𝔚𝔞𝔰𝔥𝔦𝔫𝔤𝔱𝔬𝔫 𝔓𝔬𝔰𝔱

Mr. Johnson, looking slimmer than he did in office and with his hair more silvery....

- New York *Post*,
  Nov. 16, 1972

Ruddy-faced, white-haired, and heftier about the middle now, the 36th President of the U.S.....

- New York Times,
  Nov. 16, 1972

RINSE HAIR

Always rinse hair after swimming to prevent drying.

- *Spokane Daily Chronicle*

The main on Main Street broke again. The break appears to be a mystery. The pipe is only 40 years old, Sheiffer told the board and should last 100 years. All breaks are occurring at off-peak hours, Sundays or early mornings. Sheiffer indicated that the cause may be mental fatigue which would require a rethreading of the main (put a new pipe inside the old one.)

- *Concord* (Mass.) *Patriot*

Yesterday morning all trains were met by the Greenbrier's limousines and taken directly to the hotel for breakfast.

- New York Times

Deaf viewers with the signal decoding device will see the picture with the captions; to others the TV picture will appear exactly as it does not.

- Boston Globe

The Indian Government is of the view that more than a military approach a diplomatic initiative taken by the countries of the region would pave the way for a Soviet withdrawal from Moscow.

- *Indian Express*

"You couldn't talk to a nicer guy (than Taylor)," said Mrs. Doris Lauer, who lived across the street from the Taylors.
  "You never would have thought he had mental problems," she said, asking not to be identified.

- *Detroit Free Press*

CORRECTION

JULIA CHILD - In some editions yesterday, the ingredients of Duxelles included "2 tablespoons liquor." It should have read "2 tablespoons flour."

- *New York Post*

At Homowack Lodge, he met his wife, Roberta, while serving her as a waiter. The romance flourished and terminated in marriage $3\frac{1}{2}$ years ago.

- *Brooklyn Trump
  Village News*

Mussels give up a good deal of their own liquor as they cook and this is one of the finest broths known to any cook. Or to anyone who dies on them.

- *Sunday Cape Cod Times*

A British reference during debates to George Orwell's book *Animal Farm*, as an illustration of the need felt by some governments to control the flow of information, evoked a surprising response from a Soviet delegate during the European Human Rights debate, here. He said that *Animal Farm* was about Britain and had nothing to do with the Soviet Union.

— *The Times*, London

He declared the small business man is being "squeezed" by the Republican Administration.
Housewives, he noted, are concerned about rising prices.

— New York Times

Yesterday's first leader in *The Times* concerned people who try to stamp on ideas they don't like. "High Court judges do it frequently", it thundered.
By the second edition the paper had decided that High Court judges did no such thing. It was "tin pot dictators" who did it frequently.

— *The Guardian*

Meanwhile, the Commerce Department's report on durable goods was seen an an encouraging sign that the economy may finally be ending.

— *Post-Register*
Idaho Falls

Pacific Gas and Electric Co. reported hundreds of minor outrages throughout Northern California as the wind caused short circuits and branches were blown onto the lines.

— *San Francisco Chronicle*

There was a home-from-home Shakespearean touch to the end of the Queen's Danish State visit when she sailed into Elsinore in the Royal Yacht *Britannia*. There is a Hamlet Hotel, although it is not commercialised.
The Queen was told that before Viking times there had been a dithery Amleth from Jutland. This was according to Saxo Grammaticus, a Danish chronicler.

— London *Daily Telegraph*

Born in Miners Mills, Pa., Mr. Siley lived in Palisades Park for the past 50 years. He was a driver for the Bergen County Board of Chosen Freeloaders.

— *The Dispatch*,
Hudson/Bergen Counties
New Jersey

The Assemblymen also were miffed at their Senate counterparts because they have refused to bite the bullet that now seems to have grown to the size of a millstone to the Assemblymen whose necks are on the line.

— New York Times

Richmond, Va., Aug. 13 - Frank Moran, secretary-treasurer to the state police superintendent, told this one today: A rookie state patrolman, feeling his authority, stopped a tourist car which was several inches out of the right highway lane.

"Where are you from?" he demanded.

"Cincinnati," replied the tourst.

The new officer smiled triumphantly. "Well, buddy, suppose you explain why you've got Ohio tags on your car."

-Associated Press,
August 13, 1937.

There is nothing a cop likes better than to catch someone in a lie. Our favorite instance of this sort is the time a traffic policeman in the town on North Woodstock, New Hampshire, stopped a car for speeding. The driver was a woman.

"Where are you from?" the cop demanded "Philadelphia," replied the lady.

The copy put on a wise look and nodded his head.

"Oh, so you're from Philadelphia, eh?" he said sarcastically. "Well, if you're from Philadelphia, whatcha doin' with them Pennsylvania license plates?"

- *The New Yorker,*
August 21, 1937.

(Radio newscast opening tease just after late arrival of bulletin announcing the death of Indian prime minister Jawaharlal Nehru)

"GANDHI IS DEAD." (pause) "AND SO IS NEHRU."

- Ron Nessen,
NBC NEWS

Marjorie Evans was slightly bruised Monday afternoon when a car struck her in front of the bank. George Baker, the driver, picked her up, and feeling her all over to make sure no bones were broken, insisted on taking her home where he could make a closer examination.

- *Norwood* (Ohio)
Enterprise

Our paper carried the notice last week that Mr. Herman Ogle is a defective in the police force. This was a typographical error. Mr. Jones is, of course, a detective in the police farce.

- *Ootlewah* (Tenn.) *Times*

The book is nicely printed and contains few typographical errors; however, it is strange that the proo readers should rave permitted "Lay on MacDuff" to come out "Law on Macduff."

- *Fairmont West Virginian*

Mrs. Parker Converse has the honor to announce the marriage of her daughter Patricia Converse McDonald to Mr. William James McDonald, Jr., on Saturday, December 18th.

The ceremony was performed by the family minister, Rev. Ernest Cockrell, and took place in Mr. and Mrs. McDonald's new home on Converse Point, which they will move into after a brief wedding trip.

Witnesses were Mr. and Mrs. C. Angus McDonald, and Mr. George Heath, who was installing plumbing in the house at the time.

- *Marion* (Mass.)
Sippican Sentinel

(WASHINGTON) --- PRESIDENT NIXON TODAY PROCLAIMED MAY "OLDER AMERICANS MONTH," SAYING THE NATION "POSSESSES NO GREATER NATURAL RESOURCE THAN THE COLLECTIVE WISDOM AND EXPERIENCE" OF ITS SENIOR CITIZENS. IN A SECOND PROCLAMATION, NIXON ALSO DESIGNATED MAY AS "NATIONAL ARTHRITIS MONTH."

- United Press International

CORRECTION

Due to a typographical error, the meaning of Gail Sheehy's final assessment of Phyllis Schafly's leadership style in Monday's People section was inadvertently altered. The final paragraph should have read: "Today unencumbered by empathy on a personal level or by the democratic process on a political level, Phyllis Schafly is brilliantly success-ful as a moral boss. There is but one fatal flaw in her style of leadership. If she is run over by a truck, there are no survivors."

In Monday's edition, the word "no" was omitted in the final sentence.

- Orlando Sentinel Star

Thousands of people living in the valley and along the slopes of the surrounding mountains fled their homes and headed into Kabul by bus, cart and donkey, but the witnesses said Soviet and govern-ment troops refused to let them enter the capital except on the first day. This was done to avoid the influx of a large number of refugees into Kabul, well-informed sources said.

- Atlanta Constitution

Playboy Enterprises estimates that removing ornamental

pants from its offices will save $27.000 a year.

- Knight News Wire

Q - I was recently given a bottle of walnut oil. I have no notion of what to do with it. Can you tell me?

A - A few drops applied with a soft, lint-free cloth every three months will, in all but the most stubborn cases, effectively pre-vent your walnuts from squeaking.

- New York Times

Next week when Muskie meets Soviet Foreign Minister Andrei Gromyko in Vienna, it will be the first Soviet-American exchange since the intervention in Afghan-istan last December. This meeting will offer an important opportunity for Muskie to exert a first effort toward presenting the resumption of an uncontrolled arms race.

- Michigan Daily

TWENTY-FOUL MEMBERS OF THE STRIKING PHILADELPHIA TEACHERS'

UNION WILL HAVE TO APPEAR IN COURT NEXT WEEK TO ANSWER CRIMINAL

CONTEMPT CHARGES.

- AP Radio Wire

Born in Carteret, N.J. on Nov. 4, 1911, Medwick made it to the majors when he was 20 years old and became a leader of the Cardinals' "Gashouse Gang." He compiled a career batting average of .324 with 2,471 hits including 205 homers. But he is remembered as well for his strange nickname, which came from the way he walked.

- *Newsday*,
March 23, 1975

The nickname Ducky he received when he was in the minor leagues, playing for Houston in the St. Louis Cardinals chain. A young woman spotted him splashing around a swimming pool and remarked, "He swims just like a duck." His teammates quickly called him "ducky wucky" and the name stuck.

- New York Times,
March 23, 1975

MINI-FARMS

(HARRISBURG) -- OVER IN PENNSYLVANIA, THERE'S A NEW STATE PROGRAM

DESIGNED TO TRANSFORM HUNDREDS OF PENNSYLVANIANS INTO MINIATURE,

SUBSIDIZED FARMERS. BUT SOME FARM GROUPS ARE A LITTLE EDGY.

- A P Radio Wire

Mr. Walker said an independent telephone sampling of voters nine months ago put him far ahead of Mr. Ferris and Mr. Eberhard among those who thought he would be a very good MPP. He also narrowly topped the poll of those who thought he would not be very good.

- *Toronto Globe & Mail*

Brown told the group he'll be in his office now "burning the midnight oil from 9 a.m. to 9 p.m."

- *San Bernardino Sun*

Donald Eunson, the Bedford police chief, added: "Maybe now we can dispense with justice in a more orderly manner."

- *Concord Journal*

NEXT: What happens when both husband and wife are married?

- *Cleveland Press*

Alexander's screen career began with her portrayal of James Earl Jones' wife in "The Great White Hop."

- *Milwaukee Journal*

(AUGUSTA, MAINE) -- THE PRESIDENT OF BANGOR'S STUDENT TEACHER

ASSOCIATION HAS TOLD THE LEGISLATIVE EDUCATION COMMITTEE A

QUESTIONNAIRE DISTRIBUTED TO BANGOR TEACHERS SHOWED THAT MANY

USED CAPITAL PUNISHMENT IN MAINTAINING ORDER IN THEIR CLASSROOMS.

- UPI Radio Wire

What the University of Nebraska Foundation needs is for more people to die who have remembered the foundation in their wills, foundation Chairman D.B. Varner said Tuesday.

- Lincoln Star

Nor incidentally is poverty the cause of the increase in the crime rate since 1960. Poverty fell during the Great Depression and during three recessions in the 1960s; it boomed during the prosperous 1960s.

- David J. Frum,
Yale Daily News

"In this country demand for gasoline has slowed down even though prices are still going up."

- Ray Brady, CBS News

On Aug. 30, 1901 a special train carrying Vice President Theodore Roosevelt stopped at the station to give a 10-minute speech before heading to Springfield.

- Bloomington-Normal (Ill.)
Daily Pantagraph

"And those who love nostalgia will now have to look to the future."

- Howard Cosell,
ABC SPORTS

Gail Roy Fraties, Hohman's attorney, put his hands over his eyes when the verdict was announced. He rested his other hand on Hohman's shoulder.

- Juneau Empire

(STORY IN ITS ENTIRETY)

GRANITE CITY, ILL. (UPI) - In the early 1970s, a mysterious foe of pollution known only as "The Fox" once showed his contempt for industrial pollution by pouring sludge on a steel executive's office carpet.
Officials say "The Fox" may have struck again.

NEXT, THE MAGAZINE OF THE FUTURE (708 Third Ave., New York, NY 10017) has suspended publication.

- The Writer

PREVIEWS & REVIEWS ...

Paul Buck, a poet from West Yorkshire, ended his performance by making himself vomit -- a graphic comment open to many interpretations.

- Newsletter of Greater London Arts Association

IGNORANCE: A CASE FOR SCEPTICISM
Peter Unger, Professor of Philosophy,
New York University 1975 21.5 x 14
cm   336 pages
Clarendon Library of Logic and Philosophy
₤6.50

The author argues for his view that, not only can nothing ever be known, but no one can ever have any reason at all for anything. A consequence of this is that we cannot have realistic emotional ties to anything: no one can ever be happy or sad about anything. Finally, he argues that no one can ever believe, or even say, that anything is the case. English, he suggests, and any language like it, embodies a theory about the nature of things which leads inevitably to these paradoxical conclusions. To put things right, we must depart radically from our present linguistic habits.

- *Some New Oxford Books*
on Philosophy

...the best I have ever seen, with David Waller's virile bottom particularly splendid.

Clive Barnes's review of
A Midsummer Night's Dream
- New York Times

...the best I have ever seen, with David Waller's virile Bottom particularly splendid.

- Later Edition

JOSEPH BEUYS COYOTE
Caroline Tisdall, published
Schirmer/Mosel   ₤7.50

A photographic documentation of a staged confrontation with a coyote containing 140 enigmatic and some menacing pictures of a shrouded Joseph Beuys in a barren room with a mystified, rather endearing coyote. There is a very brief text by Caroline Tisdall, irritatingly in German, but the images cannot really be strengthened with words anyway.

Arnolfini Program,
London

Another aspect of language is that it contains history. For instance some German writers who call themselves the Group of 47 came together in 1947 sharing the view that the way in which the German language had been used during the Nazi period had polluted it. Phrases like "the final solution" could no longer be used in the language. "Strength through joy" no longer meant strength through joy, but something else. If you were going to write in German again, you had to break the language down to start again. It was a very brave process and out of it came much of the great postwar, German literature.

Now the British won the war, or at least they failed to lose it. As a result, although they lost their empire, no such examination of imperialist attitudes within British society and the English language ever took place. No such attempt as the Germans made to remake the English language for the postcolonial world was ever undertaken. As a result, writers in Africa and the Caribbean, as well as India, are very conscious of the need to decolonize not only their societies but also the language they use.

- Salman Rushdie
UNESCO FEATURES

The truly original event of the month is sculptural and takes place mostly in the Richard Demarco Gallery where the Romanian artist, Illie Pavel, is showing four of the haunting pieces he has made during a four-month stay on a farm just outside the city. Fashioned of clay, rope, wood and manure, these big environmental symbols are all poetry, illuminating Truth with a methaphor.

- Edward Gage,
Arts Review,
London

Hilton is at his most playful when his spiky forms take on an ambiguity that can transform them into a cow or a cheeky heap of dung.

- Caroline Tisdall,
The Guardian

...always there was a stance of distance, a juxtaposing of the realistically painted sheen of stockings and high-heeled shoes with areas of paint which insisted on their presence and role as paint.

- Paul Overy,
The Times,
London

I much enjoyed a second helping at the Crane Kalman gallery of the poetic visions of Mary Newcomb, a lyrical innocent who injects a genuine glow-worm glimmer of inspiration in her muzzy little evocations of pastoral joys.

- Nigel Gosling,
The Observer

The interest is frankly, even rabidly sexual. When characters take off their pants they have parts that dangle impishly. As the camera pans over a roofscape, the very rats are observed screwing. A male virgin quakes with horrified anticipation as a huge whore subsides all over him with a blissful kiss. A male hustler shrills with delight as a duped client beats the lilac daylights out of him.

But the energy generated, the witty observation, the absolute perfection of racial or social accents on the soundtrack, the elliptical speed of the story, the plethora of inventiveness, the marvellous sophistication of design, above all the constant running commentary of implicit criticism - all of this makes the film not only enjoyable but defensible.

- Alexander Walker
London *Evening Standard*

UnPublished

NOVELS

CHICKENSHIT (A MORAL ISSUE)

By A. Alexandra, Los Angeles, CA

What we have here is a one-joke story about Syd, who runs a market that sells paper chickens. In the end, when a gang invades his shop, demanding chickens, and learns the truth, Syd is shot dead, along with his dog Charlie. The title of the manuscript accurately describes the story. L.J.

*- West Coast Review
of Books*

"Sixty Minutes," Channel 3 at 6 p.m., will include reports on the high cost of getting Alaskan oil to the "Lower 48," radiation pollution caused by everything from highway speed traps to kitchen microwave ovens and Woody Allen.

- Wisconsin State Journal

She sings, oh Lord, with a rowdy spin of styles - country, rhythm and blues, rock, reggae, torchy ballad - fused by a rare and rambling voice that calls up visions of loss, then jiggles the glands of possibility.

- Time

The completion of the finest concert of this season was Debussey's "La Mer." Here the Maestro's finely spun understanding of the work gave much more nuance to the orchestral colors, rhythms, dynamics and chiaroscuro than are commonly heard. The final movement was so vivid as to be able to see the whitecaps and feel the mal de mer.

- Webster (N.Y.) Post

Mastroianni, who originally wanted to become an architect, is a frugal man who lives in a million-dollar villa on Rome's Appian Way. The son of a carpenter, he is surrounded by servants, an Ethiopian liveryman and half a dozen gardeners.
He owns four sports cars and a valuable art collection but seems even at his age to be devoted primarily to beautiful women.

- Parade

Beverly Mann Padgett, 29, plays the lead role as Maria. Maria is an incoragable apostulate.

- Avon Park (Fla.) Sun

"Yes," said Maggie Smith. "It was a rather difficult day. In actual fact, the dressing rooms were awash that afternoon. The plumbing went completely mad. Someone had stuffed it full of champagne corks and knickers, I think." Then Maggie Smith looked down at the Toronto *Star*. "I wonder if they even saw the play," she said rather quietly.

- The New Yorker

But what is the film saying to us? This is more difficult to answer and even after a prudent second viewing I am driven to conclude that it says nothing for the very reason that it shows everything.

- Alexander Walker
  Encounter

INTERVIEWER: Borrowing the terms employed by the Structuralists, one might say that signification is the product of the articulation of signifiers, themselves considered as non-articulated constituent elements; signification would be the unit of meaning which brings about the unification of the discontinuous data of your verbal material.

SARTRE: Exactly.

"The Writer and his Language" -
POLITICS & LITERATURE
(Calder & Boyars)

Various themes are self-evident: time, for instance, established in the first moment of the play by the sight of David Waller (Herbert) hurling walnuts at a cuckoo clock.

- Irving Wardle,
The Times, London

It is a mark of his delicacy and, dare I say, his purity, that Mr Langham makes something both lighthearted and compassionate of a song about a shepherd copulating with his sheep.

- *The Times*, London

The outstanding feature of "On Allotments" is its shape, and it is in this that its akiness to the "structural" school is discernible. The film constitutes a rigorous inscription of a chosen space (the allotment site), in the shape of a spiral.   The camera moves rightwards and down a row of lettuces.   There follows a dissolve to a lateral shot of rhubarb-stalks, again a rightward pan. Whilst the film does contain several other kinds of shot, throughout it is the rightward moving pan that dominates.   The final, memorable shot is a long encircling pan (though not a full 360°) of the borders of the site, taking in the roads, gasworks and factory plant that surround it, and complicated by being simultaneously a gradual zoom-out.

- *FILM VIDEO*,
London

MUNICH - We regret the mistake in our record of announcements of forthcoming cultural events last week which contained a typographical error. Next Monday the National Theatre in Munich will be putting on a performance of *"Salome"* (the opera by Richard Strauss) and not *"Lou Salome"* (the psychoanalyst and friend of Sigmund Freud).

- *Suddeutsche Zeitung*

The L.A. premiere of "Hair" was as big a smash as the one in New York. This marvellous movie has to go through the roof. Of course, half the seats were roped off for 400 of Producer Michael Butler's intimate friends.

- *New York Daily News*

THE SOCIALISED PENIS

Jack Lietewka

A Rising Free Reprint 10pp 5p

Jack Lietewka did not have an erection on three separate occasions 1970-71, when he was with women he liked, who liked him, and with all signals apparently set at go on both sides. In this short pamphlet he attempts to account for these apparently isolated instances. He traces the problem to the fact that his penis was "socialised" to respond to women only in terms of "objectification, fixation and conquest." It therefore "failed him" in situations that lacked these trappings of lust and seduction. A woman friend interpreted the same data rather differently, suggesting that Lietewka had, to a certain extent, liberated himself, but was not capable of treating women as sexual equals, and rejected them totally rather than give up "the last bastion of male supremacy."

The Socialised Penis comes over as an honest piece of self-criticism, aimed at male rather than female readers. His account of male sexual initiation is specific to the US, but could provide a useful basis for discussion in this country. He doesn't offer easy solutions, rightly recognising that the process of socialisation is not easily reversed.

Available from Rising Free, 197 Kings Cross Road, London WC1.

- Christopher Roper,
Spare Rib

As a whole the *LORD OF THE RINGS* must be accounted, above all, a triumph of onomatopoeia, the ultimate exploration of the moral suggestiveness of the syllable.

- Richard Luckett,
Spectator

Josipovici's metaphors range from stripping and tattooing to obesity, drowning and the piling-up of garbage, and his poetry is that of a late 20th-century Lewis Carroll whose Alice must wait for Godot when she wants so intensely to get to Sidcup.

- John Mellors,
The Listener,
London

We have in these poems a venture into modes of sensibility and compassion which will play their limited yet crucial note in the re-fructifying of society itself.

- Terry Eagleton,
The Tablet

...the moment when he compels the girl to accompany the act of buggery with a stream of associative obsenities surrenders language to the id with a power that is Dada-esque in its intensity.

- Alexander Walker
Encounter

In an advertising blurb for In the Spirit of Crazy Horse, *a new book by Peter Matthiessen, Leonard Peltier writes, "I would like to encourage everyone to read this book, especially those who are concerned about human rights. The same ad points out that Peltier was "convicted of murdering two FBI agents in a brutal shoot-out."*

- *TIDBITS & OUTRAGES*
The Washington Monthly

The Absolute, the cruel companion of Jarry's fantasies, momentarily relented, permitting waking thoughts. In the passage above, a female becomes a woman; in another, the ferocious visions of men wedded to hyperbolic bicycles yield their secret origin, in what Pascal called the heart. Ellen Elson explains to her lover, "The Absolute Lover must exist, since woman can conceive of him, just as there is but one proof of the immortality of the soul, which is that man, through fear of nothingness, aspires to it!"

- John Updike,
The New Yorker

After a 1978 G-rated film starring Jimmy Osmond flopped, the next Osmond film, "Going Coconuts," starring Donny and Marie was PG.

One character was killed on screen to win the rating. "We found a lot of people were offended at that," said Crutchfield. "They couldn't believe the Osmonds would make anything other than a G film. But when you see it, it's so cute and so hilarious you see it's done in good taste."

- *Monterey Peninsula Herald*

I was wrong, and I can't really imagine what all those church groups were protesting about (this being an era when a person cannot even bicycle to his or her church group without having to run a gantlet of so-called adult movies and magazines, most of which now seem to be featuring small crippled children, Eurasian dental assistants, and kangaroos)...

- Michael J. Arlen,
The New Yorker

She calls her novels "histerotics." "It's the sex that drags the reader through history," she said. Her last novel, *Fountain of Glory*, set in the Middle Ages, opens with a naked maiden being chased by two hunters. She tries hard to make the "banal interesting."

- *Chariot*
Mira Costa College

Eileen Simpson, a former wife of poet John Berryman, has done a study of creativity in poets and has been a clinical psychologist. Her authority in this novel is impeccable. Her sense of bewilderment and anguish is beautifully created, and it is impossible to read. "The Maze" without being deeply and permanently moved.

- New York Times

Even if the music was largely disappointing, the show was never dull. If one tired of hearing about the dreams, gypsies, crystal visions and white birds that make up the spacy lyrical world of Stevie Nicks, one could still have fun just watching her perform.

In no less than five different costumes over the course of the night, all ruffles and flowing capes, Nicks twirled and dipped and shivered across the stage as if happily lost in an enchanted forest. No doubt she treads a fine line between uninhibited artistic expression and self-indulgent weirdness, but she manages to carry it off without being laughable because it is obvious that she is merely being her own fascinatingly flaky self.

- Washington Times

Once in a while, like a thirst for oozing fruit, the palette craves a fine romantic novel.

- Jill Weldon,
Vogue

The second Kidsplay at the Tate Gallery, which opens on Tuesday, is an ambitious attempt to transform six of the gallery's best-known paintings into giant playgrounds. Matisse's abstract "L'Escargot" is translated into a huge three-dimensional jigsaw composed of the same shapes and colours; a pinball like machine which tosses paint in buckets inside relates to a Pollock; and Van Gogh's life is taught by means of a wooden climbing structure with steep hills, a plateau and a sudden suicidal drop.

BRIEFING,
- The Observer,
London

The basic schema of the new paintings is that one large rectangle of pure colour is set off against another with a wide variety of related commotions in margins and on edges; within that schema, visitors will find a new puissance of feeling.

- John Russell,
Sunday Times,
London

Ursula Le Guin's vision of the multiverse has a sibylline austerity; the Redgrove-Shuttle dreamscapes and phantasmagoria are a very different kettle of slippery fish. One beckons to metaphysical frontiers; the other trawls the sea-bed of the subconscious.

- Christopher Wordsworth,
The Observer

LIVERPOOL - A Scottish artist, William Turnbull, painted a blank canvas white as his entry in the eleventh John Moores art exhibit in Liverpool and took a prize of £3,000.

Eyebrows were raised when the painting was unwrapped as the 80 inch by 60 inch canvas was simply painted white with almost invisible palette strokes on it. The instructions on the back of the entry did little to help the staff who were responsible for hanging the painting because the artist had written "top" on opposing edges.

Turnbull, 56, who has exhibited all over the world, explained: "The back of the picture has 'top' written on two sides because basically both experiences are correct. It is not gravitationally oriented. It can be hung vertically or horizontally...

"A lot of my work has ambiguity - a special switch. Are you looking down or across? It may have something to do with my flying experiences in the war..." One of the judges said..."I would prefer not to say why we chose this work. Suffice it to say that Turnbull is one of the major artists in the world today and any city could could themselves lucky to have any of his paintings in their gallery."

- London *Daily Telegraph*

Today, when we read Samuel Beckett, we very often have no way of knowing which version is the original, the English or the French, and are in fact led to infer that Beckett erodes his minimalist, pellucid idiom from some immediate osmosis of both.

- George Steiner,
The Listener

Starting with the little-known Variations op. 12 on the Rondo from Herold's opera "Ludovic", he made one love the *dolce far niente*, the liquidity, the relaxed para-poetry in this early work...

A few things went amiss in the coda and in that of the C sharp minor Scherzo though here the dry, rapid left-hand counterpoint singly or in octaves tasted like delicious raw mushrooms.

- Peter Stadlen,
London *Daily Telegraph*

"The film audience is so conditioned it is doing your work for you," the film-maker explained.

At the very beginning of "Alien," Ridley Scott used this device to create unease: he makes the dialogue indistinct - so that people will be worried about what they are missing.

When the studio complained they couldn't understand what was being said, Scott said bluntly: "You're not bloody well supposed to..."

- London *Daily Mail*

The Reith Lectures on "The African Condition" by Prof. Ali Masrui, of the University of Michigan, now concluded, laid before us a whole wide domain of absurdity, rich and diversified. Its fascination is such that I cannot help returning to it.

In one of the lectures the Professor complained about the unfairness of maps of the world, which usually show Europe ABOVE Africa - a fine example of carto-graphical discrimination.

Peter Simple,
- London *Daily Telegraph*

Major Douglas Sutherland is a gentleman and he has written a comprehensive guide to what this involves.

"The gentleman," he writes, "is not fluent with such terms of endearment as 'Darling,' 'Sweetheart,' or 'My gorgeous little Passion Flower.' In moments of great affection he may refer to his wife as a 'good old bag' or 'dear old faggot' and, if she should chance to hear the remark, she will blush with pleasure and feel warm for the rest of the day."

- *The Times/Daily Telegraph*

Eleanor Coppola's "Notes" on Francis Coppola's film "Apocalypse Now" is a vivid behind-the-scenes picture of her husband's struggle to film an updated version of Joseph Conrad's "The Heart of Darkness," in which Vietnam is substituted for Africa and the Green Beret played by Marlon Brando takes the place of mad Mr. Kurtz.

She is trying to be the objective camera's eye. At the end of a brief report on her husband's birthday party - the most distinguishing features of which were that "a lot of meat fell through the grills and burned on the coals," the host ran out of cold drinks, and a cake was served that was 6-by-8-feet and decorated with a scene from "Apo-calypse Now" - she reports over-hearing the remark, "Wow, this is the most decadence I've ever seen."

- New York Times

The notorious play at the National Theatre, "The Romans in Britain", is a sell-out. How could it fail, once the whole country had been told it was chock-ful of sex and violence, nudity and obscenity? There is a real problem here for Mrs Mary Whitehouse and every-body else who objects to this kind of exhibition.

Perhaps the only answer could be to pursue the reverse tactic. Announce as loudly as possible that the next play written by Howard Brenton or produced by Peter Hall is a model of propriety, conspicu-ous for the purity of its language, the decency of its costumes and the conserva-tism of its views.

Great crowds would then stay away. And serve Messrs. Hall and Brenton right.

London *Daily Mail*

The legendary fee which Ernest Hemingway commanded in 1952 for his novella, "The Old Man & the Sea" - a hundred dollars per word - has been overtaken. A German writer, Gerhard Zwerenz, has just received 1250 DM per word. But it was not exactly a very happy transaction. Zwerenz was paid for his translation of the film script of Fellini's "Satyricon," But in the final version of the film only four words of his text were actually used.

- Die Welt

At the edges of Ian McEwan's stories there are always unspoiled boys feeding glass splinters to the pigeons, roasting budgerigars or hurling rocks at courting couples. The centres are scarely less macabre: a pus-faced chef shuts a retarded *plongeur* in his gas oven and turns on the heat; an unsuccessful actress forces her nephew to dress up, the air heavy with undefined sexual menace. Yet the beastliness is never arbitrary, and Mr McEwan's details often grow into strange, powerful images: in the title story, an oppressive tale about adolescent sex in a stewy bed-sit, he assimilates the vagina to the condition of an eel-trap.

- Julian Barnes,
New Statesman

Friday night, 2 a.m., A7 club on the Lower East side. The music is hardcore, the dance is slamming....
Suddenly the band - MOB - explodes.
Without warning, these guys erupt on the dance floor. Heads down, bodies hunkered over, arms flailing, they pound across the floor slamming into each other, the wall and the watchers.
In the dim light an ancient male ritual is being enacted which celebrates raw power and barely contained fury. The heat is up, the smell is randy, the music pounds. But the circle swirls in on itself going round a private battleground, because these young warriors have no wars to fight except an elusive recession and amorphous unease.

- Village Voice

NORMAN MAILER WRITES
HIS OWN OBITUARY

Norman Mailer passed away yesterday after celebrating his 15th divorce and 16th wedding. He was renowned in publishing circles for his blend of fictional journalism and factual fiction, termed by literary critic William Buckley "Contemporaneous Ratiocinative Aesthetical Prolegomena." Buckley was consequently sued by Mailer for malicious construction of invidious acronyms. "Norman does take himself seriously," was Mr. Buckley's reply. "Of course, he is the last of those who do..." When asked on occasion why he married so often, the former Pulitzer Prize winner replied, "To get divorced. You don't know anything about a woman until you meet her in court."

- Boston Magazine

For me the BBC's educational series "Russian - Language & People" is at its best when educating me to realise that what I had previously read as "pectopah" is actually Cyrillic for restaurant, and that "typnct" is not a typing error but translates as tourist.

Richard Last,
- London Daily Telegraph

Whatever the final score on the Oresteia trilogy (music eventually irritating, performances uneven, text at least concise, general aura interesting), the pipsqueak aftermath *Of Mycenae and Men* (BBC 2) proved that Aeschylus , even adorned by BBC fuss, is preferable to Aeschylus hardly at all. The one good joke was uttered by Diana Dors, splendid as a vast, raddled Helen. "I've had enough menages a Troy," she declared.

-London *Sunday Telegraph*

In the judgment of some entertainment executives, the relationship between TV and the motion-picture industry has come full circle. The Hollywood tycoons, in the all-time classic misjudgment of show business, at first ignored TV. They they sold off their libraries. Now they and TV are becoming partners.

- Jack Gould,
New York Times

REVIEW OF *OTELLO:*

Except for David Holloway, as the Herald, the other members of the cast were William Lewis (Casio), Jean Kraft (Emilia) and Paul Plishka (Lodovico).

- New York Times

"So You Think You Got Troubles" enjoyed a brief, bizarre life in syndication recently. This pseudo-therapeutic game show was hosted by a ventriloquist and his dummy, who promised, "We can't solve your problems," but we can get you the best advice money can buy." Three "experts" - a psychologist, a minister, and a handwriting analyst - answered such questions as, "My husband won't sleep with me anymore. Should I leave him?" Then the "contestant" guessed which expert the audience voted for. "Forty-six percent of the audience agrees with your choice, so you win $460!"
So much for decorum.

- Audrey Berman
Channels

Mr. Ives portrays the richest man in the world, a widower, who seeked social status for himself and his children.

- New York Times

A French restaurant on Forty-eighth Street in New York...came out with eggs andalouise. I thought about this for a long time and concluded that the chef spoke with an Italian accent. One day a restaurant, or gourmet, correspondent, asked him for the secret of this marvelous dish, and he replied that he got it from his Aunta Louise.

- Edwin Newman,
Strictly Speaking

Miss Farrow is an interesting personality to know more about , and her attempts to articulate her own set of faith and convictions is probably pertinent to comprehending the "Now Generation."

- Jack Gould,
New York Times

One song is very memorable. David Kernan merely sits down, his legs crossed, the smile on his face rather pale and anxiety behind his eyes, and signs very quietly" "Why can't I whistle? Everyone can whistle. I can read Greek. Easy. But why can't I whistle? I can kill dragons. But why can't I whistle?" It is the profoundest moment in a memorable evening.

— Harold Hobson,
Sunday Times,
London

When I was asked to write a few words about what the Dance Theatre of Harlem is about, I had to get the dictionary to find out what about is about. I found that this innocent little word, which we use every day, is both a preposition and an adverb. It is short, hard emphatic. It is not very beautiful, phonetically; but, poetically, it has an iambic scan coupled with infinite meaning. To be about or about something is tantamount to achievement in our moment of time and space.

— *Program for the Dance Theater of Harlem*,
London

Occasionally, when Klempere's gaunt frame, having been helped on to the platform by attendants, sits there almost immobile throughout a long movement, I have caught myself wondering whether it would make any difference if he were not actually alive; like the lifeless body of El Cid leading the armies of Christ to victory, the aura of the man would bring the evening to its triumphant conclusion.

— David Cairns
Responses,
London

As for taste, the movie is gick from one end to the other - gick like the gelatin that clings to canned ham. The maturity level is sophomore dorm, and the comedy cloys its way to detectability only occasionally on little mounds strewn across a desert of talc.

— *San Francisco Chronicle*

Writing about Michelangelo Antonioni's early films fifteen years ago, I said that "the desolate autumnal wastes of the Po Valley which Aldo aimlessly circles in *Il Grido*, the oppressive presence of the horizon, the perspectives which open on to infinity, are the exact reflection of Aldo's state of soul."
I see now that I got it the wrong way round.

— Richard Roud
Sight & Sound

In what will undoubtedly be only the first of many series of "Teaching Dogs the Woodhouse Way" (BBC) Barbara Woodhouse was to be seen teaching puppies how to poo and pee.
The dog owners were told that they could give any command they chose as long as these two activities were clearly differentiated. "I use 'Quickie!' for puddling and 'Hurry up!' for the other function." At least one viewer came close to puddling himself on hearing this, but hysteria quickly gave way to wonder. If "Hurry up!" is what she says when she wants the dog to perform the other function, what does she say when wants the dog to hurry up?
Anyway, don't be surprised if, after you have shouted at your child to hurry up, every dog in the district suddenly starts performing the other function. It will only mean that they have been trained the Woodhouse way.

— Clive James
The Observer
London

Miss Caldwell is fat and unattractive in every part of the face, body and limbs, though I must admit that I have not examined her teeth. When she climactically bares her sprawlingly uberous left breast, the sight is almost enough to drive the heterosexual third of the audience screaming into the camp of the majority. Colette had sex appeal; Miss Caldwell has sex repeal.

- John Simon,
New York

Flawlessly done, with fine performances not only by Ms. Remick but by Patty Duke Astin, Colleen Dewhurst, Tovah Feldsuch and Tyne Daly, the TV feature nevertheless has minor flaws.

- Rex Polier,
Philadelphia Bulletin

The arts in general is the main hobby of Sir John Burgh, Director-General of the British Council, according to Who's Who. Still, there's an awful lot of arts about and you can't keep up with them all, as Sir John showed during a recent visit to the British Film Institute to discuss how his council could help promote British movies abroad.
Mr Tony Smith, the BFI director, was explaining to Sir John how Chariots of Fire was the most successful British film for years.
"Chariots of what?" asked Sir John.
"Chariots of Fire,: replied Smith. "It is the most successful British film ever in the American market. It even won an Oscar."
"What is an Oscar?" asked Sir John.

- Guardian Diary

Marilyn Horne will sing the title part, with James McCracken as Don Hose.

- New York Times

Baltimore director John Waters, creator of such bizarre films as "Pink Flamingos" and "Polyester" picks his five favorite movies:

1. "All of the *Francis the Talking Mule* movies. It's the one series of movies I'm insanely jealous I didn't do. Mainly because I'd love to convince a producer to have Divine meet Francis the Talking Mule.

2. *Homicidal* by Willilam Castle. "I loved this one because they had my favorite movie gimmick, called "Chicken's Corner." They stopped the film and gave you a chance to leave and get your money back if you were too frightened. You would follow the yellow chicken footprints up the aisle as you were bathed in a yellow spotlight, and a recording intoned, 'Watch the coward...' So you were completely humiliated in front of the entire audience. It was a good movie too."

3. *The Naked Kiss* by Sam Fuller. "It's the only movie I've ever seen where crippled children jump out of wheelchairs and start to sing. It's about this prostitute that tries to go straight and she finally falls in love with a good man. Then when she kisses him, she recognizes it as the kiss of a pervert, and he turns out to be a child molester. I rented this one and showed it at my Christmas party last year."

4. *All That Heaven Allows* by Douglas Firk. "Because of the scene where Rock Hudson and Jane Wyman are finally reunited in love after he's fallen off a cliff and been crippled and everything. As they kiss, this deer wanders up to the window. It's unbelievable."

5. *Something Wicked This Way Comes*. "The 'Heaven's Gate' of the Walt Disney studios, and it also has a tornado scene in it. I automatically love any movie with a tornado scene."

- Washington Post

MORES & MANNERS...

As onetime chaplain of the Albert Schweitzer Motorcycle Club in Cincinnati, I performed marriages in parking lots with 25 motocyclists, including the bride and groom, on their bikes, who'd rev up their machines as I brought my robed arms down in benediction. I loved it all, and the fumes, and the roar as the bikers peeled off and sped up the highway...

And officiating at holy unions for same-sex couples, I recall one lesbian service where some were men and vice versa, and all inter-racial, with stunning costumes and cosmetics and harp players and strange physicalities (one bridesmaid showed me her tattoo, a green, purple and roseate snake that went like a boa from her left shoulder all around her neck and down to her belly button). It was all a wild and dignified banquet of people I didn't know existed.

Rev. Clark Wells
Unitarian Universalist World

INTERVIEW WITH DR. RICHARD ELLMAN,

DISARMAMENT PROPONENT:

The next time you hear a politician talking about nuclear war, why not vomit all over him.

"All Things Considered"
National Public Radio

INTERVIEW WITH SHIRLEY MACLAIN:

Over a 90-minute lunch, she reveals:
- Rocks have souls.
- Vegetables *may* have souls, "but I don't hear the green peppers squeak when I eat them."
- She has only one vice, "-------."
- Having a "meaningful relationship" is out. "Building connective tissue" is in.

Wait! There's more.

Her 23-year-old daughter was really HER MOTHER IN A FORMER LIFE!

- Stephanie Mansfield
𝔚𝔞𝔰𝔥𝔦𝔫𝔤𝔱𝔬𝔫 𝔓𝔬𝔰𝔱

Even though a statute is constitutional on its face, an evidentiary hearing must still be held to determine whether it is constitutional as applied to the defendant, the 11th Circuit held. Aug. 26.

In *Lamar v. Banks*, 81-7347, Joseph Lamar, an Atlanta taxicab driver, had been convicted and sentenced to one year in jail under a Georgia "fighting words" statute for saying to a female passenger "I bet your honey doesn't have the $9\frac{1}{2}$-inch penis I have." Mr. Lamar's petition for a writ of habeas corpus was denied by the District Court.

Judge Richard S. Arnold, speaking for the appeals court and sitting by designation, reversed the lower court's decision in part and remanded the case. He said that Mr. Lamar's words were not inflammatory per se. Since there was no trial transcript to show precisely what evidence the fact finder had heard, Mr. Lamar deserved a new hearing, Judge Arnold concluded.

- *The National Law Journal*

Family doctor Riyaz Syed fell out of love with his wife, and into love with a pin-up. He became obsessed with the scantily-clad Indian woman in the picture, the divorce court judge said yesterday.

One of Dr Syed's hobbies was painting and he drew a large portrait of the girl in the magazine "continually painting and repainting the face and breasts," said Sir John Arnold, president of the High Court Family Division. He gave the wife, Mrs Hoora Syed, a decree nisi because of her husband's unreasonable behaviour.

London *Daily Mail*

Last night defense counsel Evseroff went wearily home after the third full day of cross-examination through which he has struggled to portray Miss Melanie Cain as a Circe turning men into swine, a thesis upon whose plausibility his client, murder-suspect Buddy Jacobson's only real chance would seem to] hang.

At one point yesterday, perhaps his highest, Evseroff managed to elicit from Miss Cain the courtroom concession that, in one of their several last farewells, she may have dismissed Jacobson in language roughly translatable as "Get the Carnal Knowledge out of Here, You Anal Cavity."

Time was when words so vulgar on lips so soft would have affronted the gently-nurtured; but enough Romeos get themselves directed hence by enough Juliets in such terms these days as to make almost our age's equivalent for "Parting is such sweet sour."

- Murray Kempton
New York Post

A coalition of vegetarians and wildlife preservationists has just the advice that many homeowners in the New York metropolitan area have been waiting to hear this summer: Don't mow the grass.

If the people leading this campaign have their way, the verdant lawns of New York, New Jersey, and Connecticut will soon turn to wild meadows.

"We must do what we can to save the grass," said Nellie Shriver of Takoma Park, Md., a leader of the effort, the so-called plant rights campaign.

The campaign was begun six years ago by a vegetarian lobbying group called the Fruitarian Network. The idea of letting lawns grow wild has since gained informal support from leaders of wildlife and religious organizations...

Miss Shriver...said the stop-mowing effort had nearly 6,000 vegetarian followers. The Fruitarians eat mostly fruit and believe in nonviolence toward living things, including lawn grass and the small creatures that live within it.

- New York Times

There have been so many great parties at Studio 54....The first really glamourous one was Halston's birthday party for Bianca Jagger. Only a hundred were invited, and the highlight of the party came when a naked black boy led a naked black girl on a white pony out from behind a curtain of gold streamers. They were covered in gold dust.

Halston gave Elizabeth Taylor a great birthday party there too. The Rockettes wheeled out an enormous birthday cake baked in the shape of Elizabeth. She blew out the candles.

- Andy Warhol,
Book Digest

In Sacramento, California a jury has awarded $142,000 to the mother of a man whose corpse was pilfered and romanced by apprentice embalmer Miss Karen Greenlee, 23, a natural recruit for the Mother Jones constituency if she is not already a subscriber or actual staff member. The court decision itself is a chilling one, vexing to advocates of sexual freedom, to feminists, and to those of us who have long championed an end to the senseless prosecution of victimless crimes. There had been growing confidence among progressives that the proscription of acts committed between consulting adults might finally be overthrown, but the Greenlee decision is a definite setback and source of sadness to necrophiliacs who have long held that their quiet pleasures represent a perfectly normal sexual preference, much like homosexuality. Unfortunately, now that court proceedings reveal that Miss Greenlee had made sexual liaison with as many as forth other corpses whilst employed by the Sacramento Memorial Lawn mortuary, it will be very difficult for progressives to argue that promiscuity is unnatural to necrophiliacs or that they are capable of warm, lasting relationships. The case was also very damaging to proponents of Ground Zero Week whose whole point was to establish the horror of death. Now, as Miss Greenlee's testimony makes clear, death can actually present genuine opportunities for happiness and for sexual fulfillment.

- The American Spectator

After mid-term exams are over comes a time known as the English Electives period. Theoretically this is a time when one can break away from one's "regular" English course to take a course of one's own choice. This year most of the electives being taught are new to GFS. The most popular new course was Peter Reinke's Man and Woman. Originally three large sections of the course were planned, but one was cancelled to allow Mr. Reinke to teach a section of Guilt.

- Earthquake,
Germantown Friends School

London - A girl of 14 told an Old Bailey jury yesterday that she and other teenagers laughed as a 13-year-old girl was tortured. She said: "She was bleeding bad. We were all laughing."

Another defendant, Bartley, refused to make a statement saying: "If I do, all the other bloods would know and I would lose my reputation. I am the tops, the main man. They do like I tell them."

- London *Daily Mail*

AGENDA ON ALCOHOL AND RELATED DISEASES, ANNUAL ADVANCED MEDICAL CONFERENCE AT THE ROYAL COLLEGE OF PHYSICIANS, HELD IN LONDON:

9:15 Alcohol in the blood
10:15 Alcohol in the liver
11:15 Alcohol in the pancreas
11:45 Alcohol in the heart
12:15 Alcoholisms
12:45 Bar opens

- Reported in
The New Yorker

The Protection of Prostitutes Bill was introduced in the House of Commons last week by Ms. Maureen Colquhoun. It is something of a triumph for the growing and vocal prostitutes' lobby as well as for its formidable spokesperson, Helen Buckingham.

Ms Buckingham has campaign tirelessly for the past four years to decriminalise prostitution and has herself "been on the game" for about seven years. She is a large woman with complete mastery of the monologue and very concerned about her public image.

In 1975 Ms Buckingham launched PUSSI (Prostitutes United for Social and Sexual Integration), which was later concerted into the more anodyne PLAN (Prostitute Laws Are Nonsense).

"We want to be seen as competent, mature people who act as sex therapists and answer a social need. We provide an alternative to women peddling desperation. That's quite a good quote."

"There are no emotional problems with us. We stop men getting tangled up with their secretaries or their best friends' wives. No, the men don't get involved ever. The act of paying out money stops all that. It's the state that's the biggest pimp of them all."

Parliamentarians believe the Bill hasn't a hope, since it must join a vast queue of other private members' Bills to get a second reading.

Ms Buckingham is undaunted. "We have to keep on fighting. It's respect we want, here. Don't put your notebook away. For too many men we have been an optical rape; a rape in the mind."

- *The Observer*,
London

HELSINKI - The Youth Board here has ruled that Donald Duck is not suitable reading for children and has cancelled library subscriptions to the comic.

The board found that Donald was unduly bourgeois. It also complained of pictures of naked ducks, tales of incomplete families, harmful attitudes towards children and Donald's common-law marriage.

- *The Times*,
London

As a woman who recently began to have "heavy spurting emissions during intercourse," I am grateful for the research being done. First, I know I'm not a freak, and second, no uninformed doctor will be able to talk me into surgery to correct "urinary incontinence" as they've done to ejaculatory women for years.

There is nothing wrong with our enjoying sex more, and I, for one, am glad I found my spot. Having this additional way to experience orgasm has enhanced my sexuality 1,000 percent. Although some men are turned off by the messy gushes (where do they get off anyway?), I wouldn't go back to dry orgasms for anyone.

- Name withheld

Ms. Magazine

INTERVIEW WITH JAMES GREY,
IMAGE CONSULTANT:

"When in doubt," he advises, "overdress." He sees people dressing up more and more all over town. "You can never be overdressed anymore, it seems. Now you can wear a tux to a picnic. They just think that you've got something important to do afterwards."

- Washington Post

AMHERST - A university study of bathroom graffiti has found that women now write on walls more than men, and their messages are "more sexual, hostile and issue-related."

These results are a striking reversal of Kinsey's famous researches into rest-room scribbling more than 20 years ago, when men wrote most of the rude words and women's graffiti was "typically romantic."

"I found the messages in women's rest-rooms very, very disturbing," said John Bates, psychologist at Amherst and co-author of the new study. "The general tone was extremely hostile, showing strong anti-male sentiment, uncertainty over how to handle men and a collapse of the romanticism Kinsey noted. One graffito we found sums it up: "Some day my prince will come. However, I'll have nothing to do with it."

Male graffiti, Bates found, is less erotic than it used to be, and more witty.

For a whole autumn, research assistants sat and copied inscriptions in Amherst rest-rooms. Bates performed chi-square analyses on the data and determined various statistical significances. Final results showed that women were responsible for 52% of all graffiti, for 62% of written responses to graffiti, and for 59% of all sexual graffiti.

In the Kinsey study only 24% of all graffiti was by women.

"This shows that the psycho-sexual hypothesis generated post hoc in the past to explain the enormously greater amount of male graffiti cannot apply to the bathroom today," Bates said. "Women are now writing most of the sexual material while men's graffiti is lighter, more humorous. This may be because women still have no social outlet for sexual innuendo."

- London _Evening Standard_

The first institute for the study of feminist thought finished its opening session with the participants, all women, doing a dance of karate kicks as a red-haired dog named Emma Goldman roamed the floor.

The dog - named for the early 20th century anarchist - belonged to the teacher of a class on "Feminism and Socialism" and the karate moves were lifted from a self-defense course.

The two classes reflect the diversity of the five weeks of lectures and discussions at the institute, named Sagaris for the double-edged sword of the Amazons representing women's strength....

Linda, a young blonde who asked that her last name not be used... said: "It's been very politicizing for all the straights and now they know they should support us instead of being ashamed of us. We are, after all, on the same side. We are all for women.

"It doesn't matter who you're in bed with if you're in bed when the revolution comes," she said.

- Burlington (Vt.) _Free Press_

Once when one of his Cabinet ministers had been arrested for committing an indecent act with a girl in Hyde Park, he (Winston Churchill) listened to the details and then said to the policeman: "You say that this happened at two o'clock in the morning?" - "Yes, sir" - "You say that the minister is over 70 years old?" - "Yes, sir" - "And you say thst the temperature was three degrees below zero?" - "Yes, sir" - "You know," said Churchill, "It almost makes me proud to be British."

- London _Daily Mail_

November 11 through the 18 marks the observance of National Childrens Book Week at the New Martinsville Public Library. On display during this time will be books for youngsters on such relevant topics as adoption, divorce, alcoholism, death, and drug abuse.

- New Martinsville (W.Va.)
Wetzel Chronicle

Normanton, Derby - An anonymous clergyman was annoyed when no one answered his knock at the door of a house, reports the parish magazine at Normanton, Derby. He left his visiting card, writing on it:
"Revelation 3, 20. Behold I stand at the door and knock; if anyone hears my voice and opens the door I will come to him."
The next Sunday a woman attended church service and gave the vicar her card inscribed: "Genesis 3: 10." The vicar looked it up and read:
"I heard the sound of thee in the garden and I was afraid, because I was naked and hid myself."

- London *Daily Telegraph*

There have been newsletters for doctors, lawyers, engineers, interior decorators, bricklayers, and joggers. Now there's one for pornographers.
"I've been into sex for a while," said Dennis Sobin, publisher of TAB (The Adult Business) Report. "Right now, I'm getting more fun than money, but I believe the money will come in." He said that he was trying to get part of the nation's multibillion dollar pronography business and that he had no competition in the field. "This newsletter will give businessmen some advice to let them know what their competitors are doing. It will let them know what's new in the business."
"Adult business" operations face different problems from other enterprises, Mr. Sobin said. "The newsletter fills a dire need on the part of adult industry businessmen who are being hounded by cops,sheriffs, politicians, tax collectors and religious zealots. They don't know how to react to fight back. Now they can exchange experiences, learn about their rights and become better managers."
Among the features of the newsletter are: (1) An editorial critical of the authorities for paying "grossly exaggerated and misdirected" attention to child pornography, (2) A collection of "news" items from around the country, including a "legal briefs" column. (3) An advertisement for postcards from Denmark and T-shirts designed for X-rated stores. (The shirts read, "Purveyors of Fine Smut since..." with blanks for the store's name and date.)
Does Mr. Solbin have any moral qualms about his endeavor?
"If I'm helping people in their business, especially small businessmen, which of these are, I feel I'm doing a moral good."

- New York Times

VAGABOND CHIC

Daniel Hechter's new fall collection, presented at the Club des Createurs in Paris a few weeks ago, is called "Pity the Poor" and features refurbished army jackets.

- *Washington Monthly*

COURT NEWS:

Steven Blake, 20, Lubec, attempted criminal mischief, attempting to throw a bottle through the passenger side window of a pickup truck owned by Stanley W. Fletcher, dismissed by state because of evidence that the attempt was not to break the window but to hit a person.

- *Bangor Daily News*

During one of the marginal sessions at the Williamsburg economic summit, delegates were reporting on developments in new technology - and initiative introduced at last year's summit in Versailles.

One report, in the clumsy language of summiteering, described progress made in "insemination" without the necessity for a male." (Not exactly a new idea, the 17th-century medic and essayist Sir Thomas Browne mused, "I would that we could propagate like trees.")

However, one of the lady interpreters in the glass booths felt that extra comment was required.   After translating the delegate's report she added - "and that's the worst news we've heard this summit."

- Financial Times

A serious study to be given to the psychology of swearing in a course being started next month by Manchester University has angered Mr Tom Normanton, Conservative M P for Cheadle, Cheshire.

A spokesman for the department said: "Swearing will be discussed on a serious level, not on trivial lines. Questions will be asked such as, 'What does it tell you about people? Is it useful in communication? Is there any class or national pattern in swearing?"

- Daily Telegraph
London

BIRMINGHAM (U.K.) - Shopgirl Amanda Rigby's language was so fruity that she had to be sacked, her boss said yesterday. She told customers at the ladies' shoe shop to "---- off" and often used four-letter words, manageress Mrs Elizabeth Moulton told Birmingham Industrial Tribunal.

She also used a Colonel Bogey eight-letter word for part of a man's body, Mrs Moulton claimed.

But when Mrs Moulton described Amanda's swearing as "pit language" she was told to watch her words by Tribunal member Ted Lindop. Mr Lindop, a miner for 23 years, asked: "Have you ever worked down a pit?" Mrs Moulton told him "It was bad language. I probably used the wrong term."

Amanda, of Cross Heath, Newcastle-under-Lyme, Staffs, said: "I only said things like damn and bloody. I may have muttered '---- off' after an awkward customer had left the store."

The tribunal decided that Amanda's dismissal was unfair. But the members agreed she was half to blame and reduced her compensation to £170.

Tribunal chairman Mr Donald Rigbey said: "I swear and I dare say everyone in this room swears from time to time."

After the hearing Mr Lindop said: "I have heard worse language since I left the pits than I ever did when I was down there."

- The Sun, London

From PETER YOUNGHUSBAND
in Cape Town

The South African Government has just ruled that the recipient of any gonad transplant may not use his new organ for procreation - unless he gets permission from the Minister of Health and Welfare.

A gonad is a gland, either testes in males or ovaries in females, which contains cells involved in reproduction and which produce sex hormones.

But as transplant surgery in South Africa has not yet progressed to reproductive organs, the new law appears to be the theoretical work of far-sighted legislators...

The pioneer heart transplant surgeon, Professor Christiaan Barnard, ducked the issue when approached by a reporter. "I've never transplanted a gonad - I'm only into hearts," he said.

- International Herald Tribune

SEATTLE, July 21 (AP) - Beverly Bonnell says she was fired as a front desk clerk at the YMCA because she refused to shave off her small, wispy black beard.

"This is a Christian organization and they don't understand the body God gives you," Bonnell, 23, said. "Our Creator gave us the bodies we have and we should try to love them and take care of them the best we can."

Bonnell's work evaluation lists "excessive hair growth" as a flaw in her work performance and supervisor Vivian Katagion said the beard was "unacceptable" to the YMCA.

But Katagion also said Bonnell was not fired, but quit, and that her work was below standard.

Bonnell said she used to shave the beard, which began growing when she was 16, but about three months ago she quit.

- Washington Post

ADVERTISEMENTS...

LIVE IN THE WOODS

Behind Old Mission -- English Tudor. Asking $185,000 for 2 Weeks

- *Santa Barbara
  News-Press*

WANTED Chairside Dental Assistant. Experienced, desirable.

- *Forest Grove* (Ore.)
  News Times

Help Wanted:

NO SHORTHAND!

A job awaits for an attractive girl of 21. Salary Ł2,300, with great fringe benefits, working to Hi-Fi Vivaldi. Hanky-panky: nil!

- *The Times*, London

Rare species, these colorful plant stakes of peeled cinnamon wood. Handcarved and painted by Sri Lanka craftsmen, each 34" tall.

- Catalogue from
  Serendipity

University of Bradford

School of Human Purposes and Communications

LECTURER IN SOCIAL PSYCHOLOGY

Applications are invited for a post in the above school. The school is a new one emphasising the inter-connections and the moral and social relevance of humanistic studies.

- *Grauniad*

(*Advertisement for
Laguna Beach hotel*)

Acres of beautiful white sand beneath your balcony and superb accomodations. Celebrated cuisine in two famous restaurants. Pool. Shopping Village. Superlative Service. Year 'round climate.

- *New Yorker*

CLASSIFIED:

An unexpected vacancy for a knife-thrower's assistant. Rehearsals start immediately.

- quoted by UPI

WANTED Berkshire County HMO Steering Committee requires an individual who has the necessary educational background and work experience to complete an objective incredible HMO Feasibility Study.

- *Pittsfield Berkshire Eagle*

FOR SALE purebred male Bug, 14 months old, loves children, excellent pet, clean, intelligent. $75.

- *Evening Times-Globe*
  St. John (N.B.)

ANTIQUES: A Nice collection of old picture frames and prints, including currier knives (Old Ford Bridge).

- Adv. *Grand Rapids Press*

LOST - 10,000 honey bees in a swarm. Do not apprehend. Call...

- Adv., *Princeton Packet*

I NEED 3 part time & 4 full time people to fill vacancies. Caused by premonitions in growing organization. High earnings & fast premonitions for hard workers.

Adv., *Schenectady Gazette*

We are proud of the part

we've played in the tremen-

dous growth of our city.

VALLEY MATTRESS

- Sacramento *Bee*

EXECUTIVE SECRETARY, (to $700) High powered engineering department needs assistant to top VIP. Dynamic, prestigious position offers exceptional reimbursement and retribution. Call Lisa Joseph, 852-5900, National Personnel, 1400 Rand Bldg. (Agency).

- *Buffalo Evening News*

LOST large White Cat. West Gleed area. May be headed for Portland, Oregon.

- *Yakima Herald-Republic*

THANK YOU

I am extremely grateful for the expression of trust and confidence shown me on Feb. 22.

I deeply appreciate your vote and will do everything in my power to betray that trust. I will be a commissioner for all the people.

Sincerely,

RALPH BURGESS

- *Panama City* (Fla.) *News-Herald*

SHEPHERDS BUSH

Pleasant maisonette, quiet street: 3 bedrooms, bath and separate w.c., large living room and dining kitchen; shared garden. Hideous entrance, needs improvement.

- *The Times*, London

In visits to Copenhagen, I found primary points of interest to be the bronze Little Mermaid in the harbor, the changing of the guard at the Royal Palace, and a good looking young chef named Jorgen Moller, who could make duck Danoise better than Cordon Bleu at his best.

Adv., Jack Kofoed,
Aloft, National Airlines

JOIN OUR HAWAIIAN ADVENTURE

8 Days 17 Nights in Honolulu

Adv. in Hendersonville (Tenn.)
Free Press & Independent News

- *Bernardsville
(N.J.) News*

- San Diego *Tribune*

- New York *Daily News*

Find out how to protect your home from a representative of the Fire Prevention Bureau of the City of San Antonio.

Adv., *San Antonio
Express-News*

Mice With Personality

To copulate a doll house or hide in your pocket.

RED PONY TOY SHOP

- *Brighton-Pittsford
(N.Y.) Post*

HAVE FAMILY, would like to exchange for home in Amsterdam.

- *International
Herald Tribune*

REPUTED EATING PLACE
AND
COFFEE SHOPPE

Prime Location. Harvard Square

- Adv., *Boston Globe*

DISSIPATIONS, PROPOSALS, RESUMES, 171's - Typed and edited, rewritten.

Adv., 𝔚𝔞𝔰𝔥𝔦𝔫𝔤𝔱𝔬𝔫 𝔓𝔬𝔰𝔱

GOLD CHAIN AND CROSS lost around Cedar Creek on June 11. Valuable momentum, reward.

- Daily Egyptian,
Southern Illinois University

St. Petersburg Opera Company, Inc.

presents

THE MIKADO
by Gilbert & Sullivan

Sung in English

- Advertisement in

St. Petersburg Times

RESPONSIBLE PERMANENT POSITION
In growing mail-order company for an articulate person, capable of working independently and composting routine correspondence.

Adv., *Lebanon (N.H.)*
Valley News

JURIED
ART EXPOSITION
AND SALE

All Artists Invited to Enter

Art Show Fri. April 11th, Sat. April 12th - 10 a.m. - 3 p.m.

All works are to be hand delivered, uncreated to Foundation building at Johonson Place in Woodmere.

- Oyster Bay Sunstorm-News

HELP WANTED

Disco Dentist needs full time Chairside Assistant for fun Brentwood ofc. Must disco or be willing to learn.

- 𝔏𝔬𝔰 𝔄𝔫𝔤𝔢𝔩𝔢𝔰 𝔗𝔦𝔪𝔢𝔰

STOP SMOKING
AS OF FEB. 13

A free class in vegetable gardening will begin Wednesday, Feb. 13 at 10 a.m. at the South Berkeley Senior Center at Ashby and King Streets in Berkeley.

- Berkeley Co-op News

- Advertisements appearing in the Buffalo Evening News, in the issues of May 9, May 14, May 16, and May 21, 1975.

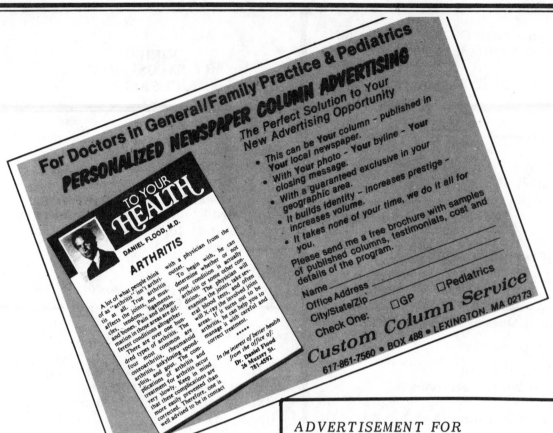
LOST - Tan Palmaranean, named "Gee" vicinity Raritan Ave. near Richmond Rd. Mon. evening 7:30 PM to 8:30 PM please return as elderly woman is attached.

- Staten Island Advance

ADVERTISEMENT FOR

UNITY FUNERAL CHAPELS, INC.:

There's so much beauty in the blooming Rose
And through its life, Who knows where it goes?
Some Roses will live over a season through
While others will enjoy part of the dew.

But even Roses with all their splendor and heart
Will one day their beautiful petals fall apart.
Man too, has his season like the Rose
And then, one day, he also must repose.

It seems incredible, in this modern day and age, with all of the great advances our society has known...with all of its technological achievements, that scientists have not discovered a new breast enlargement method.

- Breast Enlargement & Waist Reduction
by Craig Stratton

(Ad-Images, 1982)

WORLD WAR II ALMANAC 1931–1945:
A Political and
Military Record

496 pp. 7¼ x 9¼

Hardbound Ed.
Pub. at $0.00

This Softbound Ed.
ONLY $10.95

- Publishers Central Bureau

SAVE REGULARLY IN OUR BANK.

YOU'LL NEVER REGET IT.

> *- Clifton Forge (Va.)*
> *Daily Review*

POTOMAC PLAZA APT. - Very nice
effic. on top floor. Fully equipt. kit.,
lovely view. All the inconveniences.
Call Mrs. Masak.

> *- Advertisement in*
> the Washington Post

WANTED - A mahogany living room
table, by a lady with Heppelwhite legs.

> *- Atlanta Journal*

BUY YOUR FANCY NECKLACES

DIRECTLY FROM THE MANUFACTURER -

100 PER CENT CHEAPER.

> *- Paris Herald*

For Rent: Front room, suitable for
two ladies, use of kitchen or two gentlemen.

> *- Hartford Times*

At last! After years of intensive study
for the concert stage, I am now prepared
to offer my services as an accomplished
male baby-sitter.

> *- The Village Voice*

FOR SALE

BLACK BEAR RUG. North American.
Fur excellent condition. Was a movie star.

> *- Los Angeles Times*

Jointer-Plane - used once to cut off
thumb. Will sell cheap.

> *- Long Beach Tri-Shopper*

Pair Adjustable Crutches, used one
month, $5. Roof shingles, new, $2 bundle.

> *- Bayside (N.Y.) Selling Post*

Tombstone slightly used. Sell cheap.
Weil's Curiosity Shop.

> *- Philadelphia Inquirer*

Unemployed diamonds for sale at big
discount. New four-diamond wedding ring.
Slightly used seven-diamond engagement
ring. Bought in burst of enthusiasm for
$550, sentimental value gone, will sacrifice
for $250.

> *- La Marque (Texas)*
> *Times*

Gelding - spirited but gentle. Ideal
for teen-ager. For sale by parents
whose daughter has discovered boys
are more interesting than horses.

> *- Grand Rapids Press*

I have finally figured out the right message for my answering machine - I'm out right now, when you hear the beep, please leave a message." I used to run on and on explaining my absence, urging the caller to record...people hung up before I got to the end! My favorite magazine put me on to this wonderful machine. They said it was better to <u>know</u> he hadn't called while you were out walking the dog than pretend he might have and live on (fake) hopes for two weeks! I love that magazine. I guess you could say I'm That COSMOPOLITAN GIRL.

- Advertisement,
Cosmopolitan

Position Wanted:

AM I YOUR MAN?

I am a proven winner in sales of high ticket, prestige products and services.
I am a tenacious and creative professional with that delusive ability to deliver the bottom line.

Advertisement,
Wall Street Journal

INFLATION GOT YOUR $DOLLARS$

MUNROE & SONS CONSTRUCTED HOMES CAN GIVE YOU QUALITY AT TOMORROW'S PRICES

- *Kitsap County* (Wash.) *Herald*

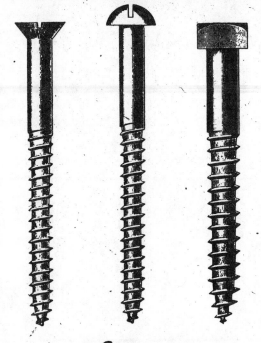

CLARK AVE. - Sunny 2 story home, 3 Bedrooms, 1½ baths, FPL, large enclosed offers waterviews, near Yale Boasting Club.

— Advertisement,
New Haven Register

TRAINEE

Major Abstract and Title Co. located near downtown Miami is looking for a bright and vicious person to train as credit manager, handling collections, etc. Must have own transportation.

Advertisement in
the *Miami Herald*

INCOME TAX

FORMS DONE

1040-EZ, $5. Other forms charged by complicity.

— Advertisement, *Cincinnati Northeast, Suburban Life*

Creole Delicacies from Old New Orleans

STRAWBERRY PRESERVES

Fraise de la Louisiana, sun-ripened whole fruit in a pure preserve of incompatible flavor.

— Advertisement in the
National Observer

New and Outrageous!

Now, after months of studying consumer behavior, rigorous marketing research, and final testing, the Saturday Evening Club is proud to announce a new bumpersticker:

I ♣ BABY SEALS

Designed to provoke. Certain to infuriate. Guaranteed to annoy. This bumpersticker is available exclusively through the Saturday Evening Club.

[$2 each, or 3 for $5, postage paid.] Send your order to The Saturday Evening Club, P.O. Box 877, Bloomington, Indiana 47402.